Easy to Use

PICK UP & PLAY
COMPLETE
BEGINNERS
CHORDS
FOR GUITAR

SEE IT ▦ HEAR IT

JAKE JACKSON

CW00539305

Flame Tree Music

mobile
online
in print

Flame Tree Music
BOOKS • eBOOKS • RESOURCES

Contents

Publisher/Creative Director: Nick Wells • Layout Design: Jane Ashley
Website and Software: David Neville with Stevens Dumpala and Steve
Moulton • Project Editor: Gillian Whitaker

First published 2019 by
FLAME TREE PUBLISHING
6 Melbray Mews, Fulham,
London SW6 3NS, United Kingdom
flametreepublishing.com

Music information site: flametreemusic.com

19 20 21 22 23 24 25 • 1 2 3 4 5 6 7 8 9 10

The CIP record for this book is available from the British Library.

ISBN: 978-1-78664-273-9

All images and notation courtesy of Flame Tree Publishing Ltd, except the following guitar diagrams
© 2019 Jake Jackson/Flame Tree Publishing Ltd. Courtesy of Shutterstock.com and © the following
contributors: Busjia 9; Studio 72 19; Aedka Studio 35; Matyuschenko 137; 141 Pepsco Studio; Emotions
studio 143; aprilante 155; Shannon West 157; Syda Productions 172.

Every effort has been made to contact copyright holders. We apologize in advance for any omissions and would be pleased to insert the appropriate acknowledgement in subsequent editions of this publication.

Android is a trademark of Google Inc. Logic Pro, iPhone and iPad are either registered trademarks or trademarks of Apple Computer Inc. in the United States and/or other countries. Cubase is a registered trademark or trademark of Steinberg Media Technologies GmbH, a wholly owned subsidiary of Yamaha Corporation, in the United States and/or other countries. Nokia's product names are either trademarks or registered trademarks of Nokia. Nokia is a registered trademark of Nokia Corporation in the United States and/or other countries. Samsung and Galaxy S are both registered trademarks of Samsung Electronics America, Ltd. in the United States and/or other countries.

Jake Jackson (author) is a writer and musician. He has created and contributed to over 30 practical music books, including Guitar Chords and How to Play Guitar. His music is available on iTunes, Amazon and Spotify amongst others.

Thanks to Alan Brown (for some of the musical examples)

Printed in China

Complete Beginners Chords for Guitar
An Introduction

For any guitarist, chords are vital for playing music with understanding and flexibility. With just a few chords it is possible to learn hundreds of songs, so knowledge of the most popular chords can get you a long way. In this book you'll find:

1. A chord section containing the most common chords: **majors**, **minors**, **sevenths** and **sus4** chords in all 12 keys.

2. **Alternative positions** for all major and minor triads, again with clear diagrams showing the fretboard, strings to play, and suggested fingering.

3. A quick guide to what chords are and how they are used, covering the **different types** of chords that exist and their relation to keys, scales and other chords.

4. A section devoted to chords in context, introducing more **advanced** chord types and examples of **simple chord progressions** to get you started with putting chords together.

5. General advice on **playing chords** and finding ways round difficult chord shapes and combinations.

It's important to keep practising until you're familiar with the basics and ready to move on. This book provides a good start: as well as clear and simple chord diagrams, there are handy reference tables and tips for jazzing up your chord technique and style. Plus, if you get stuck there are also links throughout to our extensive audio library of chords and scales at **flametreemusic.com**.

The Diagrams
A Quick Guide

START
HERE

THE
BASICS

A

A#/Bb

B

C

C#/Db

D

D#/Eb

E

F

F#/Gb

G

G#/Ab

CHORDS IN
CONTEXT

The majority of diagrams in this book are for chord shapes, though there will also be some examples of notes written in standard and TAB notation:

Standard Notation

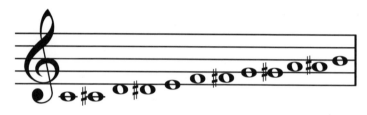

C   C#   D   D#   E   F   F#   G   G#   A   A#   B

TAB Notation

Some guitarists prefer to use tablature (called TAB) instead of staves. The six lines represent the six strings of the guitar, from the high E string to the low E string, and the numbers represent the frets that produce the notes. A zero indicates that the string is played open. In the below example, the first C is played on the 5th string – the A string – by holding down the third fret along.

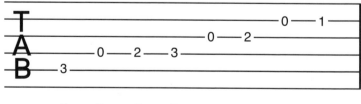

C   D   E   F   G   A   B   C

FREE ACCESS on iPhone & Android etc, using any free QR code app

Scan to **HEAR** the C major chord, and access the full library of scales and chords on flametreemusic.com

Chord Diagrams

The Strings: The bass E appears on the left (6th string).
The top E is on the right (1st string).
The top E is the E above **middle C** on the piano.

Fingerings:

E A D G B E

1 is the index finger   **2** is the middle finger
3 is the ring finger   **4** is the little finger

String isn't played   Open string position   Nut at the top of the neck

X   O

The 1st fret*

Finger position for the notes

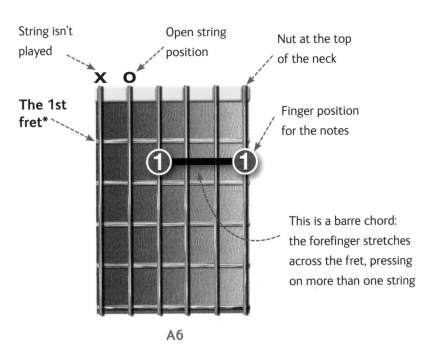

This is a barre chord: the forefinger stretches across the fret, pressing on more than one string

A6

* When the chord position isn't as close to the nut, a number to the left indicates the changed location on the fretboard. E.g. a '2' means the diagram starts from the 2nd fret rather than the 1st.

FREE ACCESS on iPhone & Android etc, using any free QR code app

Scan to **HEAR** the C major chord, and access the full library of scales and chords on flametreemusic.com

THE BASICS
A
A#/B♭
B
C
C#/D♭
D
D#/E♭
E
F
F#/G♭
G
G#/A♭
CHORDS IN CONTEXT

START HERE

THE BASICS

A

A#/Bb

B

C

C#/Db

D

D#/Eb

E

F

F#/Gb

G

G#/Ab

CHORDS IN CONTEXT

The Sound Links
Another Quick Guide

Requirements: a camera and internet-ready smartphone (e.g. **iPhone**, any **Android** phone (e.g. **Samsung Galaxy**), **Nokia Lumia**, or **camera-enabled tablet** such as the **iPad Mini**). The best result is achieved using a WIFI connection.

1. Download any **free QR code reader**. An app store search will reveal a great many of these, so obviously it's best to go with the ones with the highest ratings and don't be afraid to try a few before you settle on the one that works best for you. Tapmedia's QR Reader app is good, or ATT Scanner (used below) or QR Media. Some of the free apps have ads, which can be annoying.

2. On your smartphone, open the app and **scan** the **QR code** at the base of any particular page.

FREE ACCESS on iPhone & Android etc, using any free QR code app

Scan to HEAR the C major chord, and access the full library of scales and chords on flametreemusic.com

3. Scanning the chord will bring you to the C major chord, and from there you can access and hear the complete library of scales and chords on flametreemusic.com.

FREE ACCESS on iPhone & Android etc, using any free QR code app

Scan to **HEAR** the C major chord, and access the full library of scales and chords on flametreemusic.com

THE
BASICS

A

A#/B♭

B

C

C#/D♭

D

D#/E♭

E

F

F#/G♭

G

G#/A♭

CHORDS IN
CONTEXT

In the chord section, the QR code at the bottom of those pages will take you directly to the relevant chord on the website.

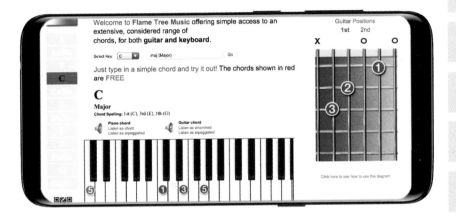

4. Use the drop down menu to choose from **20 scales** or 12 **free chords** (50 with subscription) per key.

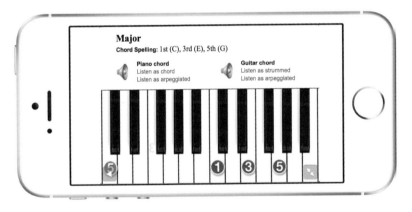

5. Click the sounds! Both piano and guitar audio is provided. This is particularly helpful when you're playing with others.

The QR codes give you direct access to chords and scales. You can access a much wider range of chords if you register and subscribe.

FREE ACCESS on iPhone & Android etc, using any free QR code app

Scan to **HEAR** the C major chord, and access the full library of scales and chords on flametreemusic.com

START
HERE

THE
BASICS

A

A#/Bb

B

C

C#/Db

D

D#/Eb

E

F

F#/Gb

G

G#/Ab

CHORDS IN
CONTEXT

The Basics

As the building blocks of music, chords play an important role in any guitarist's repertoire. The sheer amount of different chords that exist can be daunting for a beginner, but this book is designed to help you identify which ones are the most useful and learn how to play them.

Most popular songs are formed using just a few chords, as there are particular types of chords that sound better together. Understanding the relationship between chords and the notes within them is the best way to know which ones to play and when. The chord section of this book, which starts on page 40, lays out the most popular chords for each key, but to accompany that this chapter introduces the basic concepts behind chord construction.

As well as handy reference tables, this chapter includes definitions and diagrams to illustrate common terms.

This section will cover:

- **The guitar fretboard and chord symbols**
- **The relationship between chords, keys and scales**
- **Construction of chords**
- **Chord types within this book explained**
- **Common chords in each key**
- **Hand position, playing technique and plectrum use**
- **Open chords and barre chords**
- **Options for tackling difficult chords**

FREE ACCESS on iPhone & Android
etc, using any free QR code app

Scan to **HEAR** the C major chord, and access the full library of scales and chords on flametreemusic.com

START HERE

THE BASICS

A

A#/Bb

B

C

C#/Db

D

D#/Eb

E

F

F#/Gb

G

G#/Ab

CHORDS IN CONTEXT

FREE ACCESS on iPhone & Android etc, using any free QR code app

Scan to **HEAR** the C major chord, and access the full library of scales and chords on flametreemusic.com

START
HERE

THE
BASICS

A

A#/Bb

B

C

C#/Db

D

D#/Eb

E

F

F#/Gb

G

G#/Ab

CHORDS IN
CONTEXT

The Fretboard

It's always useful to have a clear idea of where each note lies in relation to other notes. On the guitar, the frets are organized in semitone intervals.

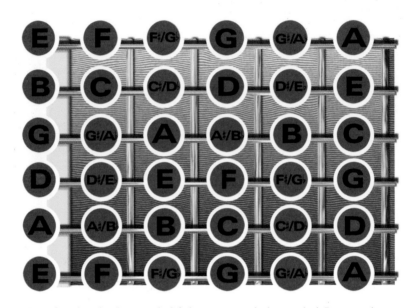

Guitar fingerboard with nut on the left, bass strings at the bottom, high E string at the top

Because the guitar has a three to four octave range, and some notes can be played at exactly the same pitch in several **fingerboard positions**, the harmonic possibilities on the instrument are almost endless: even simple major or minor chords can be played in numerous fingerboard positions – each with a multitude of possible fingerings.

Use shapes that suit your fingers and that work well with the other chord shapes you're playing. Often you'll find that, rather than having to jump around the fingerboard to play the next chord in a song, you can devise an **alternative fingering** near to the previous chord.

FREE ACCESS on iPhone & Android etc, using any free QR code app

Scan to **HEAR** the C major chord, and access the full library of scales and chords on flametreemusic.com

What Is a Chord?

A chord is simply different notes sounded together. In their most basic form, they are formed of three notes. When chords are combined they are called a chord progression.

Below is a diagram of the C major chord. This is a great chord to start with, as it contains no sharps or flats. It is an example of a **triad**: made of three notes, it consists of a root note (C), third (E) and fifth note above (G). The notes played on the guitar from left to right according to this diagram would be:

unplayed string; C; E; G (open string); C; E (open string)

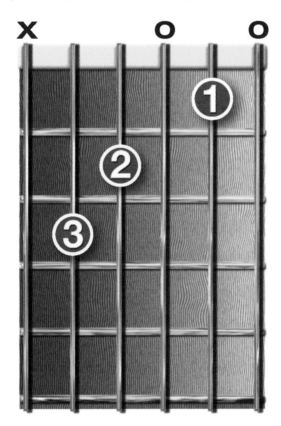

START HERE

THE BASICS

A

A#/Bb

B

C

C#/Db

D

D#/Eb

E

F

F#/Gb

G

G#/Ab

CHORDS IN CONTEXT

FREE ACCESS on iPhone & Android etc, using any free QR code app

Scan to **HEAR** the C major chord, and access the full library of scales and chords on flametreemusic.com

START
HERE

THE
BASICS

A

A#/Bb

B

C

C#/Db

D

D#/Eb

E

F

F#/Gb

G

G#/Ab

CHORDS IN
CONTEXT

Chord Symbols

There are two main types of chords that form the core of most popular music: major chords and minor chords. The distinguishing feature between these relies on the 'third', or middle note of the triad.

Major Chords

The chord symbol that tells you when to play a major chord is simply the letter name of the chord written as a **capital**. For example, the chord symbol for the G major chord is 'G'; and the chord symbol for the D major chord is 'D'. Major chords have a **bright, strong** sound.

Minor Chords

Minor chord symbols consist of the capital letter of the chord name followed by a **lowercase 'm'**. For example, the chord symbol for the E minor chord is 'Em' and chord symbol for the A minor chord is 'Am'. Minor chords have a **mellow, sombre** sound.

Other Chords

Although there are dozens of different chord types that exist in music, all of them stem from the basic major and minor triads. Other chord types tend to just extend or vary the notes of the major or minor triads using other notes from the key.

Opposite, the most common chord types and their symbols are shown for the key of C. Not all of these chord types are present in this book, but being able to recognize the symbols will be useful, as they tell you which notes from the key are needed to form the chord.

FREE ACCESS on iPhone & Android
etc, using any free QR code app

Scan to **HEAR** the C major chord, and access the full library of scales and chords on flametreemusic.com

Chord Name	Chord Symbol	Chord Notes
C major	C	C, E, G
C minor	Cm	C, E♭, G
C augmented triad	C+	C, E, G♯
C diminished triad	C°	C, E♭, G♭
C suspended 2nd	Csus2	C, D, G
C suspended 4th	Csus4	C, F, G
C 5th (power) chord	C5	C, G
C major 6th	C6	C, E, G, A
C minor 6th	Cm6	C, E♭, G, A
C dominant 7th	C7	C, E, G, B♭
C major 7th	Cmaj7	C, E, G, B
C minor 7th	Cm7	C, E♭, G, B♭
C half diminished 7th	C°7 or Cm7♭5	C, E♭, G♭, B♭
C diminished 7th	C°7	C, E♭, G♭, B♭♭
C minor major 7th	Cm(maj7)	C, E♭, G, B
C dominant 7th ♯5	C7+5	C, E, G♯, B♭
C dominant 7th ♭5	C7♭5	C, E, G♭, B♭
C major add 9	Cadd9	C, E, G, D
C dominant 9th	C9	C, E, G, B♭, D
C major 9th	Cmaj9	C, E, G, B, D
C minor 9th	Cm9	C, E♭, G, B♭
C dominant 11th	C11	C, E, G, B♭, D, F
C dominant 13th	C13	C, E, G, B♭, D, A

START HERE

THE BASICS

A

A♯/B♭

B

C

C♯/D♭

D

D♯/E♭

E

F

F♯/G♭

G

G♯/A♭

CHORDS IN CONTEXT

FREE ACCESS on iPhone & Android etc, using any free QR code app

Scan to **HEAR** the C major chord, and access the full library of scales and chords on flametreemusic.com

Common Keys

START
HERE

THE
BASICS

A

A#/B♭

B

C

C#/D♭

D

D#/E♭

E

F

F#/G♭

G

G#/A♭

CHORDS IN
CONTEXT

The **key** of a song refers to its overall tonality, and establishes the set of **pitches** (or notes) that form the basis of the work. There are **12 keys** in western music, each with a different set of pitches associated with them. Each key also has a major or minor **mode** (or version).

There are some keys that you're more likely to come across than others. Some of the most popular major keys are:

C major

D major

E major

G major

A major

These feature strongly in most of the popular music we hear around us.

The other 7 major keys are:

B major

B♭ major

C# major

E♭ major

F major

F# major

A♭ major

The table opposite lists the main basic major and minor chords, with page references to their chord diagrams in this book.

FREE ACCESS on iPhone & Android etc, using any free QR code app

Scan to **HEAR** the C major chord, and access the full library of scales and chords on flametreemusic.com

Chord Name	Chord Symbol	Chord Notes	Diagram Pages
C major	C	C, E, G	64–65
C minor	Cm	C, E♭, G	66–67
D major	D	D, F♯, A	80–81
D minor	Dm	D, F, A	82–83
E major	E	E, G♯, B	96–97
E minor	Em	E, G, B	98–99
F major	F	F, A, C	104–05
F minor	Fm	F, A♭, C	106–07
G major	G	G, B, D	120–21
G minor	Gm	G, B♭, D	122–23
A major	A	A, C♯, E	40–41
A minor	Am	A, C, E	42–43
B major	B	B, D♯, F♯	56–57
B minor	Bm	B, D, F♯	58–59

START HERE

THE BASICS

A

A♯/B♭

B

C

C♯/D♭

D

D♯/E♭

E

F

F♯/G♭

G

G♯/A♭

CHORDS IN CONTEXT

FREE ACCESS on iPhone & Android etc, using any free QR code app

Scan to **HEAR** the C major chord, and access the full library of scales and chords on flametreemusic.com

Chord Construction

START
HERE

THE
BASICS

A

A#/Bb

B

C

C#/Db

D

D#/Eb

E

F

F#/Gb

G

G#/Ab

CHORDS IN
CONTEXT

A key also tells you which scale can be used as the basis of the melody and which chords fit naturally into the arrangement. So, to understand a key it helps to look at its scale, which organizes all the notes of the key into pitch order.

Different scales produce different tonalities, but they follow patterns that can be applied to each key. The patterns take the form of a set order of **tones** (whole steps) and **semitones** (half-steps). The combination of tones and semitones tells you the distance (or 'interval') between each pitch. This combination of intervals is the same in all keys for scales of the same type.

The Major Scale

By far the most important scale in music is the **major** scale, which always follows this pattern:

T T S T T T S

When this pattern is applied to the key of C, it will produce the C major scale. Starting with C, a tone (**T**) up from C is D, then a tone up from D is E, then a semitone (**S**) from E is F, and so on. This produces the following notes:

C D E F G A B C

On the guitar, each fret is a semitone. The C major scale in standard and TAB notation is shown at the top of the next page.

FREE ACCESS on iPhone & Android etc, using any free QR code app

Scan to **HEAR** the C major chord, and access the full library of scales and chords on flametreemusic.com

START HERE

THE BASICS

A

A#/Bb

B

C

C#/Db

D

D#/Eb

E

F

F#/Gb

G

G#/Ab

CHORDS IN CONTEXT

The intervals between each note and the key note are called a '2nd', a '3rd', a '4th' etc. The **quality** of that interval is dependent on the number of semitones involved. For example, in major scales there are 4 semitones between the root note and the 3rd: this is called a **major third**.

C to D = Major Second

C to E = Major Third

C to F = Perfect Fourth

C to G = Perfect Fifth

C to A = Major Sixth

C to B = Major Seventh

If the interval distance alters, this changes its tonality and overall 'status'. For example, when 'major' intervals drop a semitone, they become 'minor'.

FREE ACCESS on iPhone & Android etc, using any free QR code app

Scan to **HEAR** the C major chord, and access the full library of scales and chords on flametreemusic.com

START
HERE

THE
BASICS

A

A#/Bb

B

C

C#/Db

D

D#/Eb

E

F

F#/Gb

G

G#/Ab

CHORDS IN
CONTEXT

Forming Triads

Chords are constructed by combining various **intervals**. Major chords, for example, are based on a **major third** interval. Using the C major scale on page 17, we can build the C major chord by taking the root note, adding the note which is a major third away from it (E), and adding the note a perfect fifth away from it (G). So, the basic notes that form a C major chord are: **C, E, G**.

It is common to number notes in a scale using **Roman numerals**, which refer to the note's position in the scale as well as the type of chord derived from it. An **uppercase numeral** means a chord built on that note is major; **lowercase** represents a minor chord.

So the scale of C major could be written as:

C	D	E	F	G	A	B
I	ii	iii	IV	V	vi	vii°
1st	2nd	3rd	4th	5th	6th	7th
Major	Minor	Minor	Major	Major	Minor	Diminished

From this we can see how the 1st (C), 3rd (E) and 5th (G) notes of the major scale give the key its **major triad**, shown by an uppercase 'I'.

Using the same method to form triads for each note of this major scale would give us a **harmonized** version of the C major scale. This shows us that the following chords are all within the key of C, as they all take their notes from the scale:

I:	C	(C, E, G)
ii:	Dm	(D, F, A)
iii:	Em	(E, G, B)
IV:	F	(F, A, C)
V:	G	(G, B, D)
vi:	A	(A, C, E)
vii°:	B°	(B, D, F)

On the guitar, although triads only contain three different notes, strumming three-string chords could result in quite a thin sound, so quite often chords are played with some of the notes **doubled** so that five or six strings can be strummed.

START
HERE

THE
BASICS

A

A#/B♭

B

C

C#/D♭

D

D#/E♭

E

F

F#/G♭

G

G#/A♭

CHORDS IN
CONTEXT

FREE ACCESS on iPhone & Android etc, using any free QR code app

Scan to **HEAR** the C major chord, and access the full library of scales and chords on flametreemusic.com

Chord Types

This book focuses on the most common chord types: **major and minor triads, 7ths (major 7th, dominant 7th, minor 7th) and sus4 chords**. The tables on the following pages list the notes for these in each key and the page references for their diagrams in this book.

Major Chords

Major chords consist of a major third interval. As seen in the previous pages, a major third is the interval from the first to the third note of the major scale e.g. in the key of C, from C to E. Major thirds are 4 semitones from the root note.

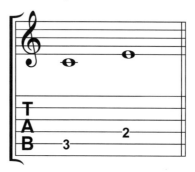

The first, third and fifth notes of the major scale make up its major triad.

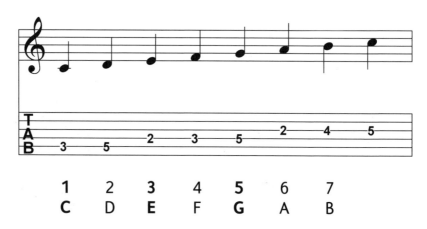

FREE ACCESS on iPhone & Android etc, using any free QR code app

Scan to **HEAR** the C major chord, and access the full library of scales and chords on flametreemusic.com

Major Triad	Notes	Diagram Pages
C	C, E, G	*64–65*
C♯/D♭	D♭, F, A♭	*72–73*
D	D, F♯, A	*80–81*
D♯/E♭	E♭, G, B♭	*88–89*
E	E, G♯, B	*96–97*
F	F, A, C	*104–05*
F♯/G♭	F♯, A♯, C♯	*112–13*
G	G, B, D	*120–21*
G♯/A♭	A♭, C, E♭	*128–29*
A	A, C♯, E	*40–41*
A♯/B♭	B♭, D, F	*48–49*
B	B, D♯, F♯	*56–57*

START
HERE

THE
BASICS

A

A♯/B♭

B

C

C♯/D♭

D

D♯/E♭

E

F

F♯/G♭

G

G♯/A♭

CHORDS IN
CONTEXT

FREE ACCESS on iPhone & Android etc, using any free QR code app

Scan to **HEAR** the C major chord, and access the full library of scales and chords on flametreemusic.com

Minor Chords

Minor triads have a more **mellow, mournful sound** than major triads but, just like major triads, they also contain only three different notes.

Minor thirds are just 3 semitones from the root note. If you **lower** the major third interval by a half step it becomes a **minor third**. Just as the major third interval determines that a chord has a major tonality, the minor third interval determines that a chord is minor.

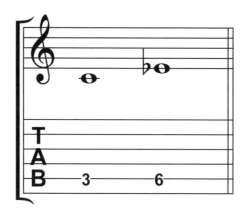

The C minor chord takes its notes from the **C natural minor scale**:

1	2	3	4	5	6	7
C	D	E♭	F	G	A♭	B♭

Scan to **HEAR** the C major chord, and access the full library of scales and chords on flametreemusic.com

START HERE

THE BASICS

A

A#/B♭

B

C

C#/D♭

D

D#/E♭

E

F

F#/G♭

G

G#/A♭

CHORDS IN CONTEXT

Major Triad	Notes	Diagram Pages
Cm	C, E♭, G	*66–67*
C#m/D♭m	C#, E, F#	*74–75*
Dm	D, F, A	*82–83*
D#m/E♭m	D#, F#, A#	*90–91*
Em	E, G, B	*98–99*
Fm	F, A♭, C	*106–07*
F#m/G♭m	F#, A, C#	*114–15*
Gm	G, B♭, D	*122–23*
G#m/A♭m	G#, B, D#	*130–31*
Am	A, C, E	*42–43*
A#m/B♭m	B♭, D♭, F	*50–51*
Bm	B, D, F#	*58–59*

START HERE

THE BASICS

A

A#/B♭

B

C

C#/D♭

D

D#/E♭

E

F

F#/G♭

G

G#/A♭

CHORDS IN CONTEXT

FREE ACCESS on iPhone & Android etc, using any free QR code app

Scan to **HEAR** the C major chord, and access the full library of scales and chords on flametreemusic.com

START
HERE

THE
BASICS

A

A#/Bb

B

C

C#/Db

D

D#/Eb

E

F

F#/Gb

G

G#/Ab

CHORDS IN
CONTEXT

7th Chords

Major seventh chords consist of a major seventh interval. This is the interval from the first to the **seventh note** of the major scale. For example, in the key of C, this would be the interval from C to B.

There are different types of seventh chords. If you lower the major seventh interval by a half step it becomes a **minor seventh**. This interval occurs in both minor 7th and dominant 7th chords. The quality of the 3rd determines whether the chord is a minor 7th or dominant 7th: dominant 7th chords include a major third, but in minor 7th chords the 3rd is minor too.

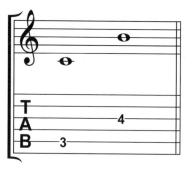 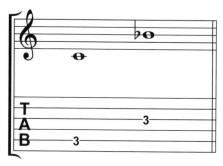

You can find the notes using the major scale, then **lower** the 3rd and 7th notes a half step if minor or dominant chords are required.

1	2	3	4	5	6	7
C	D	E	F	G	A	B

Major 7th Chords

The major 7th chord is formed by taking the basic major chord and adding the seventh note of the major scale to it. For example, Cmaj7 contains the notes: C, E, G, B.

Major 7th Chord	Notes	Diagram
Cmaj7	C, E, G, B	*page 69*
C♯maj7/D♭maj7	D♭, F, A♭, C	*page 77*
Dmaj7	D, F♯, A, C♯	*page 85*
D♯maj7/E♭maj7	E♭, G, B♭, D	*page 93*
Emaj7	E, G♯, B, D♯	*page 101*
Fmaj7	F, A, C, E	*page 109*
F♯maj7/G♭maj7	F♯, A♯, C♯, E♯	*page 117*
Gmaj7	G, B, D, F♯	*page 125*
G♯maj7/A♭maj7	A♭, C, E♭, G	*page 133*
Amaj7	A, C♯, E, G♯	*page 45*
A♯maj7/B♭maj7	B♭, D, F, A	*page 53*
Bmaj7	B, D♯, F♯, A♯	*page 61*

START HERE

THE BASICS

A

A♯/B♭

B

C

C♯/D♭

D

D♯/E♭

E

F

F♯/G♭

G

G♯/A♭

CHORDS IN CONTEXT

FREE ACCESS on iPhone & Android etc, using any free QR code app

Scan to **HEAR** the C major chord, and access the full library of scales and chords on flametreemusic.com

START
HERE

THE
BASICS

A

A#/B♭

B

C

C#/D♭

D

D#/E♭

E

F

F#/G♭

G

G#/A♭

CHORDS IN
CONTEXT

Dominant 7ths

The dominant 7th chord is formed by taking the basic major chord and adding the flattened seventh note of the major scale to it. For example, C7 contains the notes: C, E, G, B♭.

Dominant 7th	Chord Notes	Diagram
C7	C, E, G, B♭	page 70
C#7/D♭7	D♭, F, A♭, B	page 78
D7	D, F#, A, C	page 86
D#7/E♭7	E♭, G, B♭, D♭	page 94
E7	E, G#, B, D	page 102
F7	F, A, C, E♭	page 110
F#7/G♭7	F#, A#, C#, E	page 118
G7	G, B, D, F	page 126
G#7/A♭7	A♭, C, E♭, G♭	page 134
A7	A, C#, E, G	page 46
A#7/B♭7	B♭, D, F, A♭	page 54
B7	B, D#, F#, A	page 62

FREE ACCESS on iPhone & Android etc, using any free QR code app

Scan to **HEAR** the C major chord, and access the full library of scales and chords on flametreemusic.com

Minor 7ths

The minor 7th chord is formed by taking the basic minor chord and adding the flattened seventh note of the major scale to it. For example, Cm7 contains the notes: C, E♭, G, B♭.

Minor 7th Chord	Notes	Diagram
Cm7	C, E♭, G, B♭	*page 71*
C♯m7/D♭m7	D♭, E, A♭, B	*page 79*
Dm7	D, F, A, C	*page 87*
D♯m7/E♭m7	E♭, G♭, B♭, D♭	*page 95*
Em7	E, G, B, D	*page 103*
Fm7	F, A♭, C, E♭	*page 111*
F♯m7/G♭m7	F♯, A, C♯, E	*page 119*
Gm7	G, B♭, D, F	*page 127*
G♯m7/A♭m7	A♭, C♭, E♭, G♭	*page 135*
Am7	A, C, E, G	*page 47*
A♯m7/B♭m7	B♭, D♭, F, A♭	*page 55*
Bm7	B, D, F♯, A	*page 63*

FREE ACCESS on iPhone & Android etc, using any free QR code app

Scan to **HEAR** the C major chord, and access the full library of scales and chords on flametreemusic.com

START
HERE

THE
BASICS

A

A#/B♭

B

C

C#/D♭

D

D#/E♭

E

F

F#/G♭

G

G#/A♭

CHORDS IN
CONTEXT

Sus4 Chords

Some chords are formed by **replacing** a note rather than adding one. In 'sus' chords, for example, the chord's third is replaced by the **fourth** note of the major scale in sus4 chords, and by the **second** note of the scale in sus2 chords.

Of these, the sus4 chord is more commonly used, which is why we've included a version of it in the diagrams section for each of the 12 keys.

A perfect fourth is the interval from the first to the fourth note of the major scale (e.g. in the key of C, from C to F)

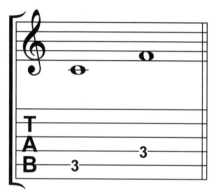

Again, you can use the major scale to find the notes:

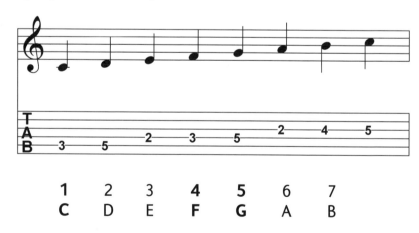

1	2	3	4	5	6	7
C	D	E	F	G	A	B

Sus4 Chord	Notes	Diagram
Csus4	C, F, G	*page 68*
C♯sus4/D♭sus4	D♭, G♭, A♭	*page 76*
Dsus4	D, G, A	*page 84*
D♯sus4/E♭sus4	E♭, A♭, B♭	*page 92*
Esus4	E, A, B	*page 100*
Fsus4	F, B♭, C	*page 108*
F♯sus4/G♭sus4	F♯, B, C♯	*page 116*
Gsus4	G, C, D	*page 124*
G♯sus4/A♭sus4	A♭, D♭, E♭	*page 132*
Asus4	A, D, E	*page 44*
A♯sus4/B♭sus4	B♭, E♭, F	*page 52*
Bsus4	B, E, F♯	*page 60*

FREE ACCESS on iPhone & Android etc, using any free QR code app

Scan to **HEAR** the C major chord, and access the full library of scales and chords on flametreemusic.com

Common Chords

Some chords within a key are more important than others. For example, the key note (the '**tonic**' – C in the key of C) is usually central to establishing the **tonality** of a section of music. You can see from the example on page 19 that there are other major triads that exist within the key of C: the **I**, **IV and V** chords are all **major triads**.

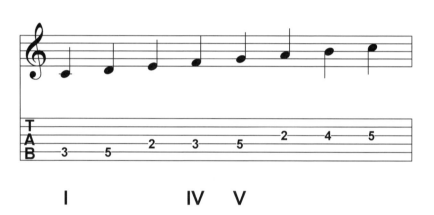

The V note (the '**dominant**') is important due to its strong harmonic relationship with the tonic. So in the key of C major, G occupies an important function and position in relation to C. Another tonally important degree of the scale is the IV (the '**subdominant**'). Chords built on any of these three notes help determine what key a piece of music is in.

Other useful chords in the key include the ii and vi chords, which are frequently found in chord progressions too. These most common chords are shown opposite in C, in standard and TAB notation.

FREE ACCESS on iPhone & Android etc, using any free QR code app

Scan to **HEAR** the C major chord, and access the full library of scales and chords on flametreemusic.com

START HERE

THE BASICS

A

A#/B♭

B

C

C#/D♭

D

D#/E♭

E

F

F#/G♭

G

G#/A♭

CHORDS IN CONTEXT

Common Chords of the C Major Scale

C Major Scale

C D E F G A B

I ii iii IV V vi vii°

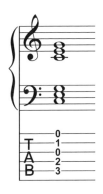

I – C Major

Notes: C, E, G

V – G Major

Notes: G, B, D

IV – F Major

Notes: F, A, C

ii – D Minor

Notes: D, F, A

vi – A Minor

Notes: A, C, E

START HERE

THE BASICS

A

A♯/B♭

B

C

C♯/D♭

D

D♯/E♭

E

F

F♯/G♭

G

G♯/A♭

CHORDS IN CONTEXT

FREE ACCESS on iPhone & Android etc, using any free QR code app

Scan to **HEAR** the C major chord, and access the full library of scales and chords on flametreemusic.com

Relative Minors

START
HERE

THE
BASICS

A

A#/Bb

B

C

C#/Db

D

D#/Eb

E

F

F#/Gb

G

G#/Ab

CHORDS IN
CONTEXT

Relative keys are keys that share exactly the same notes but have a different tonal centre (and therefore a different **tonic** note). This can be handy when moving between chords, or shifting into another key.

For example, C major and A minor are relative keys. They both contain no sharp or flat notes, but have a different tonal emphasis: A minor is a minor key, so the I, V and IV notes that would be used frequently in that key give it a different sound to I, V and IV notes used in C major. See how similar their scales are below:

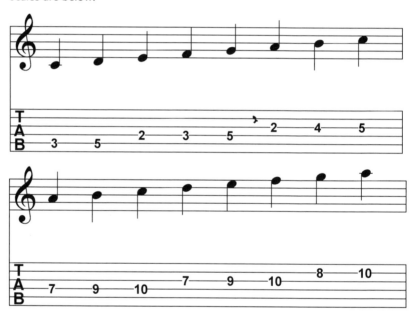

A relative minor key's note is always **three semitones below** its relative major. Or, put another way, relative minors are the **sixth degree** of the major scale (A is the sixth note of the C major scale).

The table opposite provides a quick reference of each key's relative minor, listing the minor triad notes and page references for its diagrams in this book.

FREE ACCESS on iPhone & Android etc, using any free QR code app

Scan to **HEAR** the C major chord, and access the full library of scales and chords on flametreemusic.com

Major	Relative Minor	Chord Notes	Diagram Pages
C	Am	A, C, E	*42–43*
C#/D♭	A#m/B♭m	B♭, D♭, F	*50–51*
D	Bm	B, D, F#	*58–59*
D#/E♭	Cm	C, E♭, G	*66–67*
E	C#m	C#, E, G#	*74–75*
F	Dm	D, F, A	*82–83*
F#/GA♭	D#m/E♭m	D#, F#, A#	*90–91*
G	Em	E, G, B	*98–99*
G#/A♭	Fm	F, A♭, C	*106–07*
A	F#m	F#, A, C#	*114–15*
A#/B♭	Gm	G, B♭, D	*122–123*
B	G#m	G#, B, D#	*130–31*

START HERE

THE BASICS

A

A#/B♭

B

C

C#/D♭

D

D#/E♭

E

F

F#/G♭

G

G#/A♭

CHORDS IN CONTEXT

FREE ACCESS on iPhone & Android etc, using any free QR code app

Scan to **HEAR** the C major chord, and access the full library of scales and chords on flametreemusic.com

Playing Techniques

START
HERE

THE
BASICS

A

A#/Bb

B

C

C#/Db

D

D#/Eb

E

F

F#/Gb

G

G#/Ab

CHORDS IN
CONTEXT

Hand Positions

Now that you're familiar with what chords are, it's time to start playing them! Developing the correct playing technique is important: by positioning your hands correctly, chord transitions and unfamiliar chords will be easier to master.

1. Whether playing chords or single notes, press the fretting-hand fingers as close to the fretwire as possible. This minimizes unpleasant 'fretbuzz' sounds and reduces the amount of pressure that is required, enabling you to play with a lighter, more fluent touch.

2. Try to keep all fretting-hand fingers close to the fingerboard, to minimize the amount of movement required. Your thumb should be placed at the centre of the back of the guitar neck; your fingers arching over the fretboard to descend more or less vertically on the strings.

3. Unless you are playing barre chords (see page 38) you should always use the tips of your fingers to fret notes. This will produce the sound more directly and cleanly than using the fleshier pads of the fingers.

Using a Plectrum

1. If you're using a plectrum/pick, grip it between the index finger and the thumb. Position it so that its tip extends only just beyond the fingertip, by about 1/10 in (2.5 mm), so that the amount of plectrum extending beyond the index finger is not excessive.

2. Hold the plectrum with a small amount of pressure, but be careful not to grip it too tightly as this risks losing flexibility and movement.

FREE ACCESS on iPhone & Android etc, using any free QR code app

Scan to **HEAR** the C major chord, and access the full library of scales and chords on flametreemusic.com

Strumming Techniques

Strumming chords forms the foundation of any guitar player's range of techniques. There are a couple of basic strum patterns to try on the next pages, but here are a few general tips.

1. Let the action come from the wrist rather than the elbow. A fluid and easy strumming action is best achieved this way, with the wrist loose and relaxed.

2. It's a good idea to practise in front of a mirror, or record a video of yourself playing guitar, so that you can see if you're using the right technique.

3. Be careful not to over-grip with the fretting-hand thumb on the back of the neck as this will cause muscle fatigue and tend to limit freedom of the thumb to move. The fretting-hand thumb must be able to move freely when changing chords.

4. Be aware that for the fingers to move freely the wrist, elbow and shoulder must be flexible and relaxed.

START
HERE

THE
BASICS

A

A#/Bb

B

C

C#/Db

D

D#/Eb

E

F

F#/Gb

G

G#/Ab

CHORDS IN
CONTEXT

Strumming Exercises

Minor Chords

1. Begin with E minor (page 98), as this involves only two fretted notes and uses plenty of open strings. Place your fingers on the strings, pressing lightly yet securely with the fingertips, and then strum across all six strings.

2. Strum four downstrums per measure, and then experiment by inserting a quick upstrum between the second and third beats. The upstrum should be played by an upwards movement generated from the wrist, as though the strumming hand is almost effortlessly bouncing back into position ready for the next downstrum. Keep practising this technique until it feels natural, always making sure that the arm itself isn't moving up and down when you're strumming.

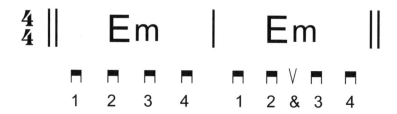

3. Once you're familiar with this chord, move your two fretting fingers from E minor to the adjacent higher strings, and add the first finger on the first fret of the B string – this is A minor (page 42). Notice that the low E string should be omitted when you strum A minor. Try the same pattern with this chord: first four downstrums, then insert a quick upstrum between the second and third beats.

4. Now you're ready to put them together: start by strumming downwards four times on an E minor chord, then without stopping change to A minor and play another four strums, keeping the same tempo. Begin the sequence again, this time adding the upstrums.

FREE ACCESS on iPhone & Android etc, using any free QR code app

Scan to **HEAR** the C major chord, and access the full library of scales and chords on flametreemusic.com

START
HERE

THE
BASICS

A

A#/B♭

B

C

C#/D♭

D

D#/E♭

E

F

F#/G♭

G

G#/A♭

CHORDS IN
CONTEXT

When you've mastered one upstrum per bar, have a go at adding two a bar:

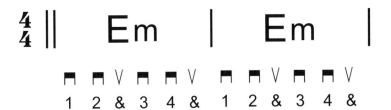

Major Chords

Next try some major chords. If G major seems like too much of a stretch between the second and third fingers, allow your thumb to move down to the centre of the back of the guitar neck until the chord feels comfortable. Notice that only the top four strings should be strummed when playing D major.

1. Begin by playing four downstrums on a G major chord (page 120).

2. Without stopping, move your fingers to D major (page 80) and play another four strums. Repeat the sequence from the beginning by changing back to G major. Notice how the third finger stays at the third fret for both G and D major. Use this as a pivot point to lead the chord change.

3. Practise slowly until you are able to change between the chords without pausing or hesitating. If you move all three fretting fingers as one shape when changing chord (rather than placing the fingers on one at a time) this will make the chord changes smoother.

4. Incorporate the same patterns of downstrums and upstrums as you did for E minor and A minor.

Turn to page 144 to see the entire sequence – E minor and A minor with G major and D major – put together.

FREE ACCESS on iPhone & Android etc, using any free QR code app

Scan to **HEAR** the C major chord, and access the full library of scales and chords on flametreemusic.com

Barre Chords

Playing open position chords is a great way to begin learning the guitar, but if you take a careful look at any professional players you'll soon notice that most of their chord positions are further up the fretboard; more often than not they'll be playing shapes known as '**barre chords**'.

Advantages of Barre Chords

Playing a barre chord involves re-fingering an open position chord so as to leave the first finger free to play the barre by fretting all six strings. The whole chord can then be **moved** up the fingerboard to different pitches.

The main advantage of barre chords is that you can move the **same shape** up or down the fingerboard to create new chords without the need to memorize a whole host of different fingerings for each chord: **a single hand position** can be used for all 12 keys simply by moving it up or down the neck of the guitar. Using barre chords will also allow you to play more unusual chords (like B♭ minor or F♯ major), which are unobtainable in open position.

Open position minor chords can also be converted to barre chords. The E minor and A minor shapes can be re-fingered to leave the first finger free to make the barre.

Here is an **A minor barre chord** based on an **E minor** shape.

Moved down to the third fret, this becomes a **G minor chord**.

Moved up the seventh fret, it becomes a **B minor chord**.

A minor
Chord Spelling
1st (A), ♭3rd (C), 5th (E)

Barre Chord Technique

Barre chords can be difficult for beginners to master, which is why we've included more than one position option for all major and minor chords in the chord section of this book. If you're tackling barre chords though, here are a few tips to develop your technique:

- **Keep the first finger straight and in line with the fret.**

- **The creases between the joints of the barring finger should not coincide with strings.**

- **Position all the fretting fingers as close to the fretwire as possible.**

- **Press down firmly, but avoid using excessive pressure.**

- **When you move between barre chords ensure that your thumb also shifts, so that your whole hand position is moving with each chord change.**

There will be some barre chords in the following chord section, often provided as alternatives to the first position major and minor triads.

With the basic ideas behind chord use now covered, you will now find diagrams for 7 of the most useful chord types in all 12 keys:

- **Major Triad: 1st and 2nd positions**
- **Minor Triad: 1st and 2nd positions**
- **Sus4 Chord**
- **Major 7th Chord**
- **Dominant 7th Chord**
- **Minor 7th Chord**

START HERE

THE BASICS

A

A#/Bb

B

C

C#/Db

D

D#/Eb

E

F

F#/Gb

G

G#/Ab

CHORDS IN CONTEXT

FREE ACCESS on iPhone & Android etc, using any free QR code app

Scan to **HEAR** the C major chord, and access the full library of scales and chords on flametreemusic.com

A
Major
(**1st** Position)

Chord Spelling
1st (A), 3rd (C♯), 5th (E)

START
HERE

THE
BASICS

A

A♯/B♭

B

C

C♯/D♭

D

D♯/E♭

E

F

F♯/G♭

G

G♯/A♭

CHORDS IN
CONTEXT

FREE ACCESS on iPhone & Android
etc, using any free QR code app

Scan to **HEAR** this chord, or go directly
to flametreepublishing.com

A
Major
(**2nd** Position)

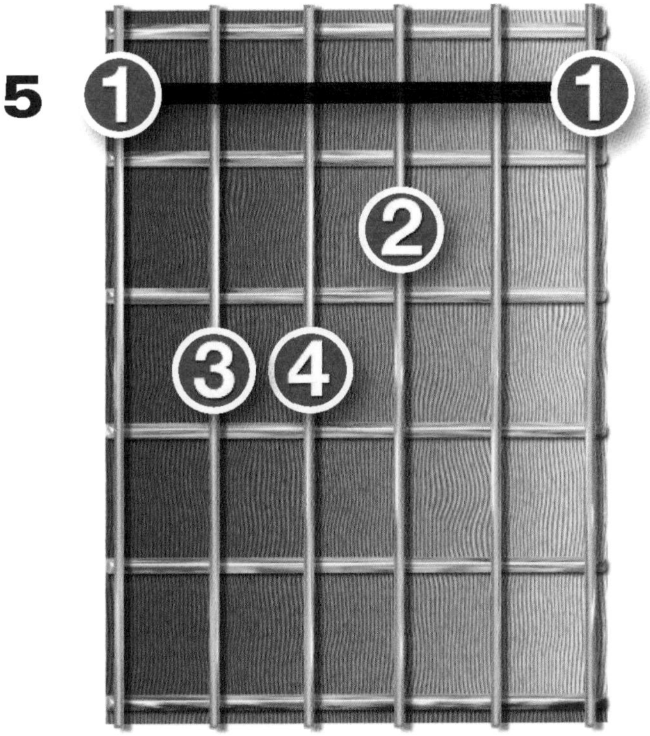

START HERE

THE BASICS

A

A#/Bb

B

C

C#/Db

D

D#/Eb

E

F

F#/Gb

G

G#/Ab

CHORDS IN CONTEXT

5

Chord Spelling
1st (A), 3rd (C♯), 5th (E)

Scan to **HEAR** this chord, or go directly
to flametreepublishing.com

START
HERE

THE
BASICS

A

A#/Bb

B

C

C#/Db

D

D#/Eb

E

F

F#/Gb

G

G#/Ab

CHORDS IN
CONTEXT

Am
Minor
(1st Position)

Chord Spelling
1st (A), b3rd (C), 5th (E)

FREE ACCESS on iPhone & Android
etc, using any free QR code app

Scan to **HEAR** this chord, or go directly
to flametreepublishing.com

Am
Minor
(**2nd** Position)

START HERE

THE BASICS

A

A#/Bb

B

C

C#/Db

D

D#/Eb

E

F

F#/Gb

G

G#/Ab

CHORDS IN CONTEXT

5

① ①

③ ④

Chord Spelling
1st (A), b3rd (C), 5th (E)

Asus4
Suspended 4th

(**1st** Position)

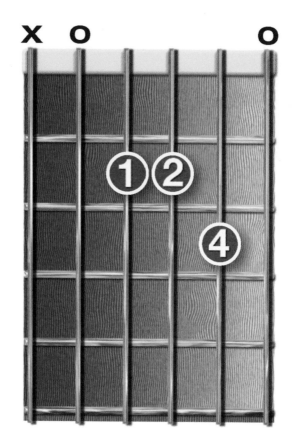

Chord Spelling
1st (A), 4th (D), 5th (E)

Scan to **HEAR** this chord, or go directly to flametreepublishing.com

START HERE

THE BASICS

A

A#/Bb

B

C

C#/Db

D

D#/Eb

E

F

F#/Gb

G

G#/Ab

CHORDS IN CONTEXT

Amaj7
Major 7th

(**1st** Position)

START HERE

THE BASICS

A

A#/Bb

B

C

C#/Db

D

D#/Eb

E

F

F#/Gb

G

G#/Ab

CHORDS IN CONTEXT

Chord Spelling
1st (A), 3rd (C#), 5th (E), 7th (G#)

FREE ACCESS on iPhone & Android etc, using any free QR code app

Scan to **HEAR** this chord, or go directly to flametreepublishing.com

A7
Dominant 7th

(**1st** Position)

START
HERE

THE
BASICS

A

A#/B♭

B

C

C#/D♭

D

D#/E♭

E

F

F#/G♭

G

G#/A♭

CHORDS IN
CONTEXT

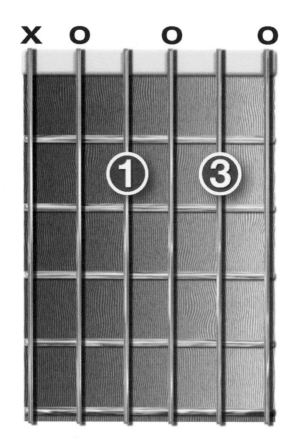

Chord Spelling
1st (A), 3rd (C♯), 5th (E), ♭7th (G)

FREE ACCESS on iPhone & Android
etc, using any free QR code app

Scan to **HEAR** this chord, or go directly
to flametreepublishing.com

Am7
Minor 7th

(**1st** Position)

Chord Spelling
1st (A), ♭3rd (C), 5th (E), ♭7th (G)

A

A♯/B♭

B

C

C♯/D♭

D

D♯/E♭

E

F

F♯/G♭

G

G♯/A♭

Scan to **HEAR** this chord, or go directly to flametreepublishing.com

47

A♯/B♭
Major

(**1st** Position)

START
HERE

THE
BASICS

A

A♯/B♭

B

C

C♯/D♭

D

D♯/E♭

E

F

F♯/G♭

G

G♯/A♭

CHORDS IN
CONTEXT

Chord Spelling
1st (B♭), 3rd (D), 5th (F)

FREE ACCESS on iPhone & Android
etc, using any free QR code app

Scan to **HEAR** this chord, or go directly
to flametreepublishing.com

A♯/B♭
Major
(**2nd** Position)

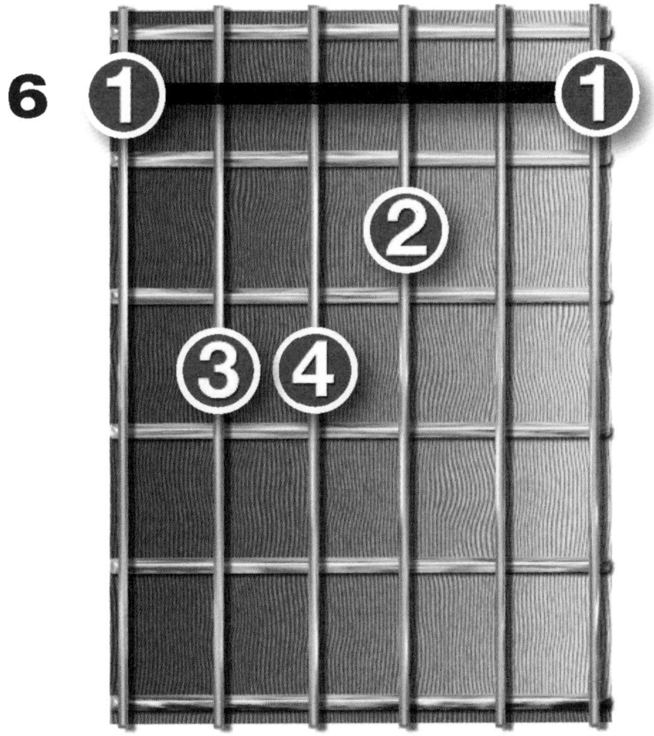

6

Chord Spelling
1st (B♭), 3rd (D), 5th (F)

Scan to **HEAR** this chord, or go directly to flametreepublishing.com

A♯/B♭m
Minor
(**1st** Position)

START
HERE

THE
BASICS

A

A♯/B♭

B

C

C♯/D♭

D

D♯/E♭

E

F

F♯/G♭

G

G♯/A♭

CHORDS IN
CONTEXT

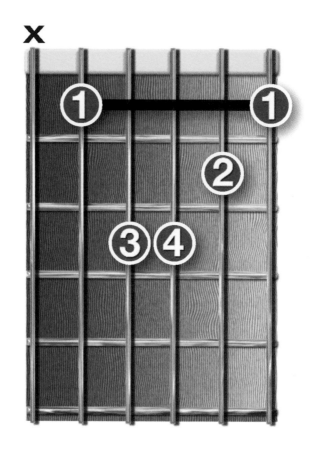

Chord Spelling
1st (B♭), ♭3rd (D♭), 5th (F)

A♯/B♭m
Minor
(**2nd** Position)

START HERE

THE BASICS

A

A♯/B♭

B

C

C♯/D♭

D

D♯/E♭

E

F

F♯/G♭

G

G♯/A♭

CHORDS IN CONTEXT

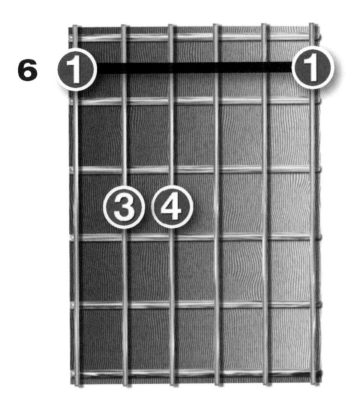

Chord Spelling
1st (B♭), ♭3rd (D♭), 5th (F)

FREE ACCESS on iPhone & Android etc, using any free QR code app

Scan to **HEAR** this chord, or go directly to flametreepublishing.com

51

A#/B♭sus4
Suspended 4th

(**1st** Position)

START
HERE

THE
BASICS

A

A#/B♭

B

C

C#/D♭

D

D#/E♭

E

F

F#/G♭

G

G#/A♭

CHORDS IN
CONTEXT

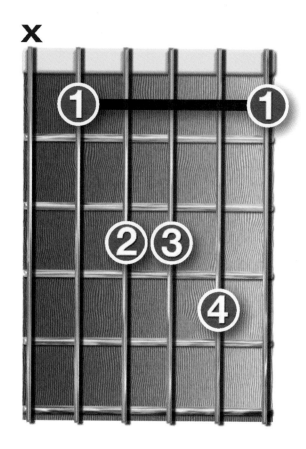

Chord Spelling

1st (B♭), 4th (E♭), 5th (F)

FREE ACCESS on iPhone & Android
etc, using any free QR code app

Scan to **HEAR** this chord, or go directly
to flametreepublishing.com

A♯/B♭maj7
Major 7th

(**1st** Position)

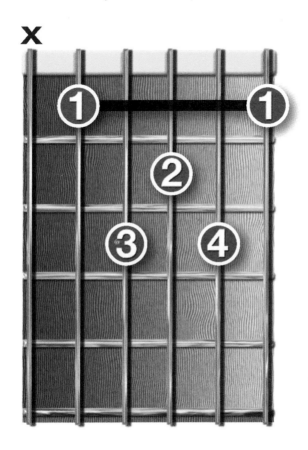

START
HERE

THE
BASICS

A

A♯/B♭

B

C

C♯/D♭

D

D♯/E♭

E

F

F♯/G♭

G

G♯/A♭

CHORDS IN
CONTEXT

Chord Spelling

1st (B♭), 3rd (D), 5th (F), 7th (A)

FREE ACCESS on iPhone & Android etc,
using any free QR code app

Scan to **HEAR** this chord, or go directly
to flametreepublishing.com

A#/B♭7
Dominant 7th
(**1st** Position)

START
HERE

THE
BASICS

A

A#/B♭

B

C

C#/D♭

D

D#/E♭

E

F

F#/G♭

G

G#/A♭

CHORDS IN
CONTEXT

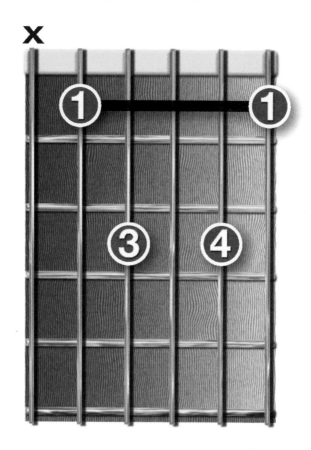

Chord Spelling
1st (B♭), 3rd (D), 5th (F), ♭7th (A♭)

FREE ACCESS on iPhone & Android
etc, using any free QR code app

Scan to **HEAR** this chord, or go directly
to flametreepublishing.com

A♯/B♭m7
Minor 7th

(**1st** Position)

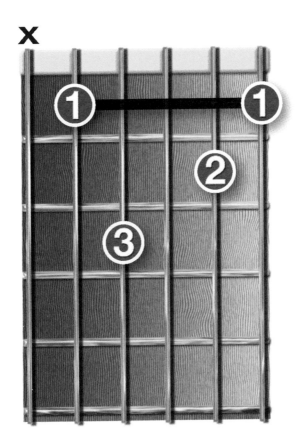

Chord Spelling
1st (B♭), ♭3rd (D♭), 5th (F), ♭7th (A♭)

FREE ACCESS on iPhone & Android etc, using any free QR code app

Scan to **HEAR** this chord, or go directly to flametreepublishing.com

B
Major
(**1st** Position)

START HERE

THE BASICS

A

A#/Bb

B

C

C#/Db

D

D#/Eb

E

F

F#/Gb

G

G#/Ab

CHORDS IN CONTEXT

Chord Spelling
1st (B), 3rd (D#), 5th (F#)

FREE ACCESS on iPhone & Android etc, using any free QR code app

Scan to **HEAR** this chord, or go directly to flametreepublishing.com

B
Major
(**2nd** Position)

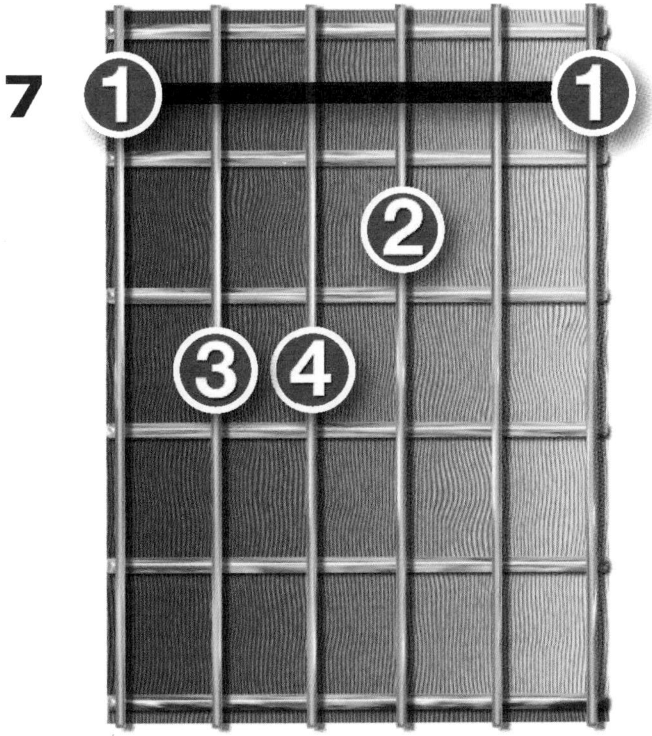

START HERE

THE BASICS

A

A#/Bb

B

C

C#/Db

D

D#/Eb

E

F

F#/Gb

G

G#/Ab

CHORDS IN CONTEXT

7

Chord Spelling
1st (B), 3rd (D#), 5th (F#)

FREE ACCESS on iPhone & Android etc, using any free QR code app

Scan to **HEAR** this chord, or go directly to flametreepublishing.com

57

Bm
Minor
(**1st** Position)

START
HERE

THE
BASICS

A

A#/Bb

B

C

C#/Db

D

D#/Eb

E

F

F#/Gb

G

G#/Ab

CHORDS IN
CONTEXT

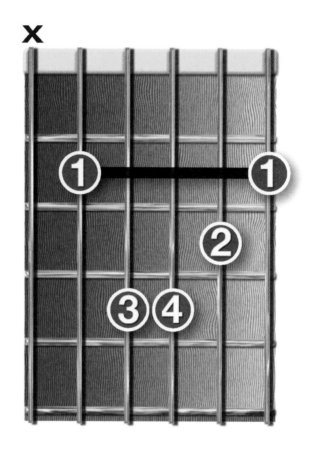

Chord Spelling
1st (B), ♭3rd (D), 5th (F♯)

FREE ACCESS on iPhone & Android
etc, using any free QR code app

Scan to **HEAR** this chord, or go directly
to flametreepublishing.com

Bm
Minor
(**2nd** Position)

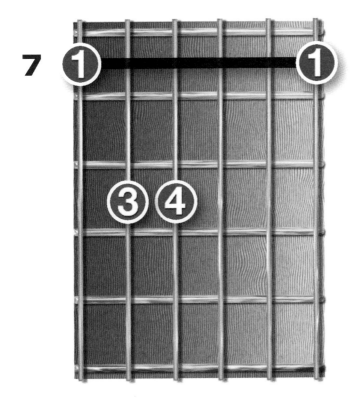

7

Chord Spelling
1st (B), ♭3rd (D), 5th (F♯)

FREE ACCESS on iPhone & Android etc, using any free QR code app

Scan to **HEAR** this chord, or go directly to flametreepublishing.com

B

Bsus4
Suspended 4th

(**1st** Position)

START
HERE

THE
BASICS

A

A#/Bb

B

C

C#/Db

D

D#/Eb

E

F

F#/Gb

G

G#/Ab

CHORDS IN
CONTEXT

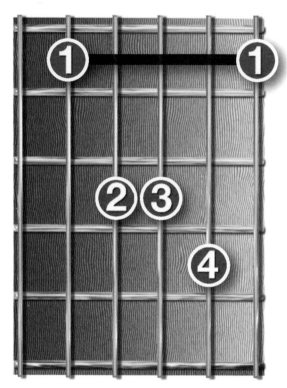

Chord Spelling
1st (B), 4th (E), 5th (F#)

FREE ACCESS on iPhone & Android
etc, using any free QR code app

Scan to **HEAR** this chord, or go directly
to flametreepublishing.com

Bmaj7
Major 7th

(**1st** Position)

START
HERE

THE
BASICS

A

A#/Bb

B

C

C#/Db

D

D#/Eb

E

F

F#/Gb

G

G#/Ab

CHORDS IN
CONTEXT

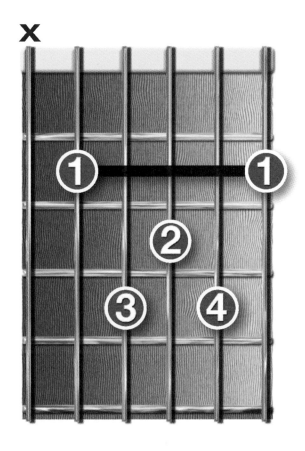

Chord Spelling
1st (B), 3rd (D#), 5th (F#), 7th (A#)

FREE ACCESS on iPhone & Android etc,
using any free QR code app

Scan to **HEAR** this chord, or go directly
to flametreepublishing.com

B7
Dominant 7th

(**1st** Position)

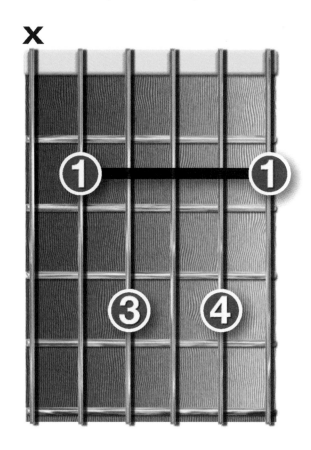

Chord Spelling
1st (B), 3rd (D♯), 5th (F♯), ♭7th (A)

Scan to **HEAR** this chord, or go directly
to flametreepublishing.com

START
HERE

THE
BASICS

A

A♯/B♭

B

C

C♯/D♭

D

D♯/E♭

E

F

F♯/G♭

G

G♯/A♭

CHORDS IN
CONTEXT

Bm7
Minor 7th
(**1st** Position)

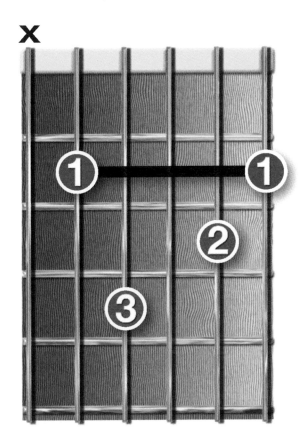

Chord Spelling
1st (B), ♭3rd (D), 5th (F♯), ♭7th (A)

C
Major
(1st Position)

START
HERE

THE
BASICS

A

A#/Bb

B

C

C#/Db

D

D#/Eb

E

F

F#/Gb

G

G#/Ab

CHORDS IN
CONTEXT

Chord Spelling
1st (C), 3rd (E), 5th (G)

FREE ACCESS on iPhone & Android
etc, using any free QR code app

Scan to **HEAR** this chord, or go directly
to flametreepublishing.com

C
Major
(**2nd** Position)

3

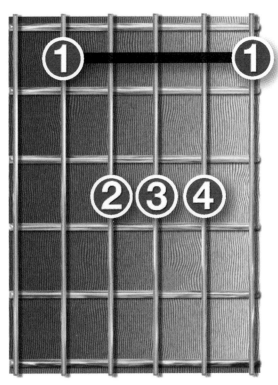

Chord Spelling
1st (C), 3rd (E), 5th (G)

Scan to **HEAR** this chord, or go directly to flametreepublishing.com

Cm
Minor

(**1st** Position)

START
HERE

THE
BASICS

A

A#/Bb

B

C

C#/Db

D

D#/Eb

E

F

F#/Gb

G

G#/Ab

CHORDS IN
CONTEXT

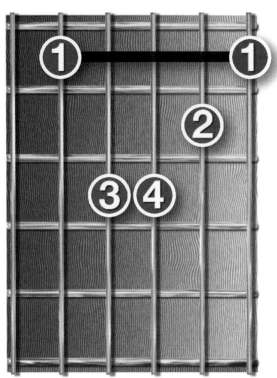

Chord Spelling
1st (C), b3rd (Eb), 5th (G)

Scan to **HEAR** this chord, or go directly
to flametreepublishing.com

Cm
Minor

(**2nd** Position)

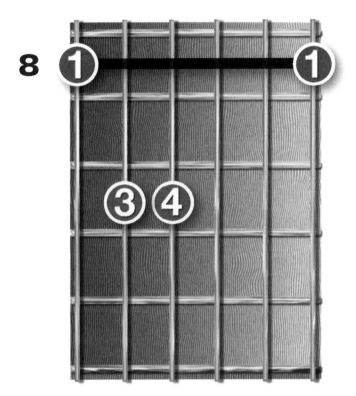

8

C

Chord Spelling

1st (C), ♭3rd (E♭), 5th (G)

FREE ACCESS on iPhone & Android etc, using any free QR code app

Scan to **HEAR** this chord, or go directly to flametreepublishing.com

Csus4
Suspended 4th
(**1st** Position)

START
HERE

THE
BASICS

A

A#/Bb

B

C

C#/Db

D

D#/Eb

E

F

F#/Gb

G

G#/Ab

CHORDS IN
CONTEXT

Chord Spelling
1st (C), 4th (F), 5th (G)

FREE ACCESS on iPhone & Android
etc, using any free QR code app

Scan to **HEAR** this chord, or go directly
to flametreepublishing.com

Cmaj7
Major 7th

(**1st** Position)

X   O   O   O

START
HERE

THE
BASICS

A

A#/Bb

B

C

C#/Db

D

D#/Eb

E

F

F#/Gb

G

G#/Ab

CHORDS IN
CONTEXT

Chord Spelling
1st (C), 3rd (E), 5th (G), 7th (B)

C7
Dominant 7th
(1st Position)

START
HERE

THE
BASICS

A

A#/Bb

B

C

C#/Db

D

D#/Eb

E

F

F#/Gb

G

G#/Ab

CHORDS IN
CONTEXT

Chord Spelling
1st (C), 3rd (E), 5th (G), ♭7th (B♭)

FREE ACCESS on iPhone & Android
etc, using any free QR code app

Scan to **HEAR** this chord, or go directly
to flametreepublishing.com

Cm7
Minor 7th

(**1st** Position)

START
HERE

THE
BASICS

A

A#/Bb

B

C

C#/Db

D

D#/Eb

E

F

F#/Gb

G

G#/Ab

CHORDS IN
CONTEXT

X

3

Chord Spelling
1st (C), b3rd (Eb), 5th (G), b7th (Bb)

C♯/D♭
Major
(**1st** Position)

START
HERE

THE
BASICS

A

A♯/B♭

B

C

C♯/D♭

D

D♯/E♭

E

F

F♯/G♭

G

G♯/A♭

CHORDS IN
CONTEXT

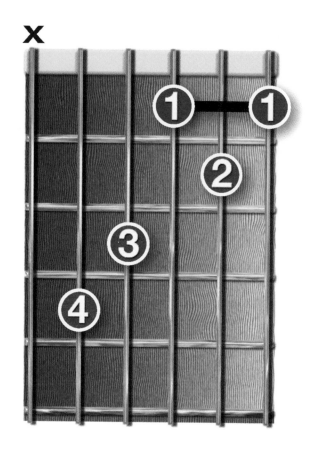

Chord Spelling
1st (C♯), 3rd (E♯), 5th (G♯)

FREE ACCESS on iPhone & Android
etc, using any free QR code app

Scan to **HEAR** this chord, or go directly
to flametreepublishing.com

C#/Db
Major

(2nd Position)

Chord Spelling
1st (C#), 3rd (E#), 5th (G#)

Scan to **HEAR** this chord, or go directly to flametreepublishing.com

START
HERE

THE
BASICS

A

A#/Bb

B

C

C#/Db

D

D#/Eb

E

F

F#/Gb

G

G#/Ab

CHORDS IN
CONTEXT

C#/Dbm
Minor

(1st Position)

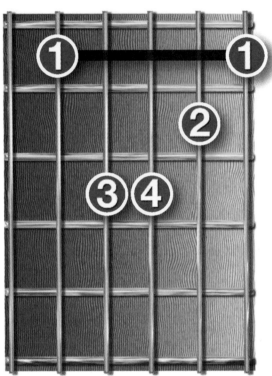

Chord Spelling
1st (C#), b3rd (E), 5th (G#)

FREE ACCESS on iPhone & Android
etc, using any free QR code app

Scan to **HEAR** this chord, or go directly
to flametreepublishing.com

C#/Dbm
Minor
(**2nd** Position)

START HERE

THE BASICS

A

A#/Bb

B

C

C#/Db

D

D#/Eb

E

F

F#/Gb

G

G#/Ab

CHORDS IN CONTEXT

Chord Spelling
1st (C#), b3rd (E), 5th (G#)

C#/D♭sus4
Suspended 4th

(**1st** Position)

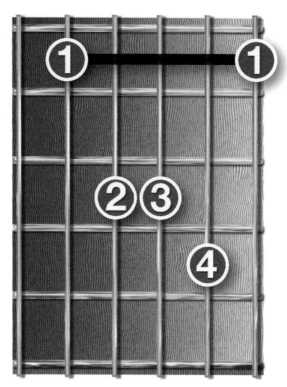

Chord Spelling
1st (C#), 4th (F#), 5th (G#)

Scan to **HEAR** this chord, or go directly to flametreepublishing.com

START HERE

THE BASICS

A

A#/B♭

B

C

C#/D♭

D

D#/E♭

E

F

F#/G♭

G

G#/A♭

CHORDS IN CONTEXT

C♯/D♭maj7
Major 7th

(1st Position)

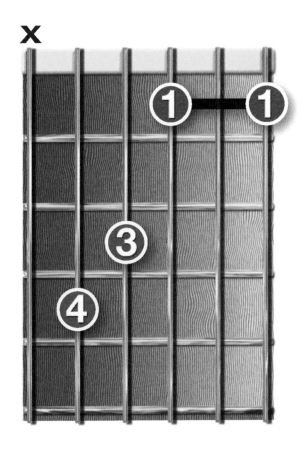

Chord Spelling
1st (C♯), 3rd (E♯), 5th (G♯), 7th (B♯)

START HERE

THE BASICS

A

A♯/B♭

B

C

C♯/D♭

D

D♯/E♭

E

F

F♯/G♭

G

G♯/A♭

CHORDS IN CONTEXT

FREE ACCESS on iPhone & Android etc, using any free QR code app

Scan to **HEAR** this chord, or go directly to flametreepublishing.com

C#/D♭7
Dominant 7th

(**1st** Position)

START
HERE

THE
BASICS

A

A#/B♭

B

C

C#/D♭

D

D#/E♭

E

F

F#/G♭

G

G#/A♭

CHORDS IN
CONTEXT

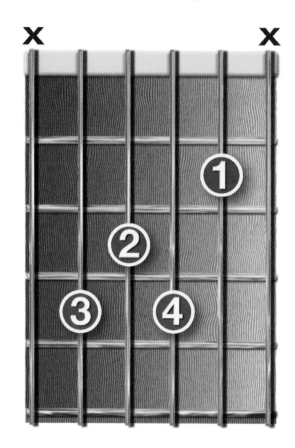

Chord Spelling
1st (C#), 3rd (E#), 5th (G#), ♭7th (B)

FREE ACCESS on iPhone & Android
etc, using any free QR code app

Scan to **HEAR** this chord, or go directly
to flametreepublishing.com

C#/D♭m7
Minor 7th

(**1st** Position)

Chord Spelling
1st (C#), ♭3rd (E), 5th (G#), ♭7th (B)

Scan to **HEAR** this chord, or go directly to flametreepublishing.com

D
Major
(1st Position)

START
HERE

THE
BASICS

A

A#/Bb

B

C

C#/Db

D

D#/Eb

E

F

F#/Gb

G

G#/Ab

CHORDS IN
CONTEXT

Chord Spelling
1st (D), 3rd (F#), 5th (A)

FREE ACCESS on iPhone & Android
etc, using any free QR code app

Scan to **HEAR** this chord, or go directly
to flametreepublishing.com

D
Major
(2nd Position)

Chord Spelling
1st (D), 3rd (F#), 5th (A)

START HERE

THE BASICS

A

A#/Bb

B

C

C#/Db

D

D#/Eb

E

F

F#/Gb

G

G#/Ab

CHORDS IN CONTEXT

FREE ACCESS on iPhone & Android etc, using any free QR code app

Scan to **HEAR** this chord, or go directly to flametreepublishing.com

Dm
Minor
(**1st** Position)

START
HERE

THE
BASICS

A

A#/B♭

B

C

C#/D♭

D

D#/E♭

E

F

F#/G♭

G

G#/A♭

CHORDS IN
CONTEXT

Chord Spelling
1st (D), ♭3rd (F), 5th (A)

FREE ACCESS on iPhone & Android
etc, using any free QR code app

Scan to **HEAR** this chord, or go directly
to flametreepublishing.com

Dm
Minor
(**2nd** Position)

X

5

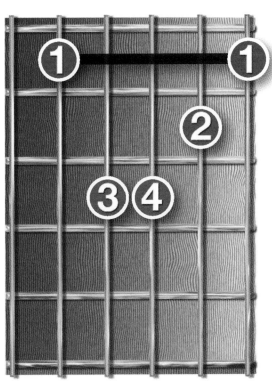

Chord Spelling
1st (D), ♭3rd (F), 5th (A)

START
HERE

THE
BASICS

A

A#/B♭

B

C

C#/D♭

D

D#/E♭

E

F

F#/G♭

G

G#/A♭

CHORDS IN
CONTEXT

Dsus4
Suspended 4th

(**1st** Position)

START
HERE

THE
BASICS

A

A#/Bb

B

C

C#/Db

D

D#/Eb

E

F

F#/Gb

G

G#/Ab

CHORDS IN
CONTEXT

Chord Spelling
1st (D), 4th (G), 5th (A)

FREE ACCESS on iPhone & Android
etc, using any free QR code app

Scan to **HEAR** this chord, or go directly
to flametreepublishing.com

Dmaj7
Major 7th

(**1st** Position)

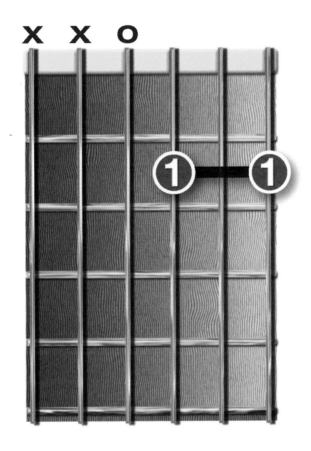

Chord Spelling
1st (D), 3rd (F♯), 5th (A), 7th (C♯)

START HERE

THE BASICS

A

A♯/B♭

B

C

C♯/D♭

D

D♯/E♭

E

F

F♯/G♭

G

G♯/A♭

CHORDS IN CONTEXT

FREE ACCESS on iPhone & Android etc, using any free QR code app

Scan to **HEAR** this chord, or go directly to flametreepublishing.com

D7
Dominant 7th

(**1st** Position)

START HERE

THE BASICS

A

A#/B♭

B

C

C#/D♭

D

D#/E♭

E

F

F#/G♭

G

G#/A♭

CHORDS IN CONTEXT

Chord Spelling
1st (D), 3rd (F#), 5th (A), ♭7th (C)

FREE ACCESS on iPhone & Android etc, using any free QR code app

Scan to **HEAR** this chord, or go directly to flametreepublishing.com

Dm7
Minor 7th

(**1st** Position)

Chord Spelling
1st (D), ♭3rd (F), 5th (A), ♭7th (C)

FREE ACCESS on iPhone & Android etc, using any free QR code app

Scan to **HEAR** this chord, or go directly to flametreepublishing.com

D♯/E♭
Major
(**1st** Position)

START
HERE

THE
BASICS

A

A♯/B♭

B

C

C♯/D♭

D

D♯/E♭

E

F

F♯/G♭

G

G♯/A♭

CHORDS IN
CONTEXT

Chord Spelling
1st (E♭), 3rd (G), 5th (B♭)

Scan to **HEAR** this chord, or go directly
to flametreepublishing.com

D♯/E♭
Major
(**2nd** Position)

START HERE

THE BASICS

A

A♯/B♭

B

C

C♯/D♭

D

D♯/E♭

E

F

F♯/G♭

G

G♯/A♭

CHORDS IN CONTEXT

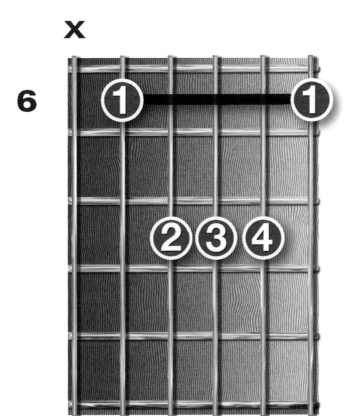

Chord Spelling
1st (E♭), 3rd (G), 5th (B♭)

FREE ACCESS on iPhone & Android etc, using any free QR code app

Scan to **HEAR** this chord, or go directly to flametreepublishing.com

D♯/E♭m
Minor

(**1st** Position)

START
HERE

THE
BASICS

A

A♯/B♭

B

C

C♯/D♭

D

D♯/E♭

E

F

F♯/G♭

G

G♯/A♭

CHORDS IN
CONTEXT

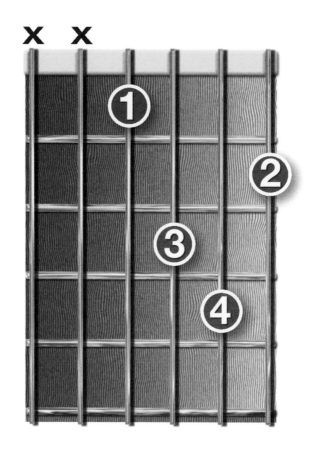

Chord Spelling
1st (E♭), ♭3rd (G♭), 5th (B♭)

Scan to **HEAR** this chord, or go directly
to flametreepublishing.com

90

D♯/E♭m
Minor
(2nd Position)

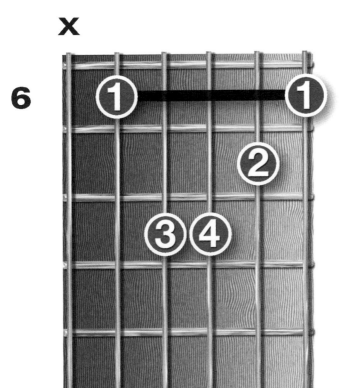

Chord Spelling
1st (E♭), ♭3rd (G♭), 5th (B♭)

Scan to **HEAR** this chord, or go directly to flametreepublishing.com

FREE ACCESS on iPhone & Android etc, using any free QR code app

START HERE

THE BASICS

A

A♯/B♭

B

C

C♯/D♭

D

D♯/E♭

E

F

F♯/G♭

G

G♯/A♭

CHORDS IN CONTEXT

D#/E♭sus4
Suspended 4th

(**1st** Position)

START
HERE

THE
BASICS

A

A#/B♭

B

C

C#/D♭

D

D#/E♭

E

F

F#/G♭

G

G#/A♭

CHORDS IN
CONTEXT

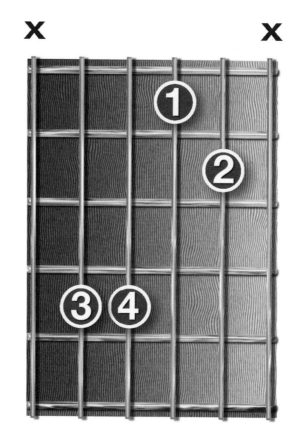

Chord Spelling
1st (E♭), 4th (A♭), 5th (B♭)

FREE ACCESS on iPhone & Android
etc, using any free QR code app

Scan to **HEAR** this chord, or go directly
to flametreepublishing.com

D♯/E♭maj7
Major 7th

(**1st** Position)

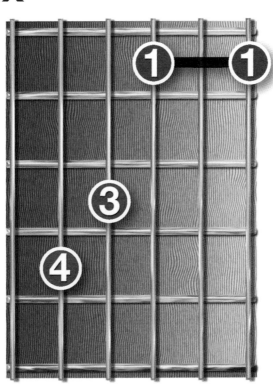

Chord Spelling
1st (E♭), 3rd (G), 5th (B♭), 7th (D)

Scan to **HEAR** this chord, or go directly to flametreepublishing.com

START HERE

THE BASICS

A

A♯/B♭

B

C

C♯/D♭

D

D♯/E♭

E

F

F♯/G♭

G

G♯/A♭

CHORDS IN CONTEXT

D#/E♭7
Dominant 7th

(**1st** Position)

Chord Spelling
1st (E♭), 3rd (G), 5th (B♭), ♭7th (D♭)

START
HERE

THE
BASICS

A

A#/B♭

B

C

C#/D♭

D

D#/E♭

E

F

F#/G♭

G

G#/A♭

CHORDS IN
CONTEXT

Scan to **HEAR** this chord, or go directly
to flametreepublishing.com

D♯/E♭m7
Minor 7th

(1st Position)

Chord Spelling
1st (E♭), ♭3rd (G♭), 5th (B♭), ♭7th (D♭)

Scan to **HEAR** this chord, or go directly to flametreepublishing.com

E
Major
(**1st** Position)

START
HERE

THE
BASICS

A

A#/Bb

B

C

C#/Db

D

D#/Eb

E

F

F#/Gb

G

G#/Ab

CHORDS IN
CONTEXT

Chord Spelling
1st (E), 3rd (G#), 5th (B)

FREE ACCESS on iPhone & Android
etc, using any free QR code app

Scan to **HEAR** this chord, or go directly
to flametreepublishing.com

E
Major
(**2nd** Position)

START HERE

THE BASICS

A

A#/Bb

B

C

C#/Db

D

D#/Eb

E

F

F#/Gb

G

G#/Ab

CHORDS IN CONTEXT

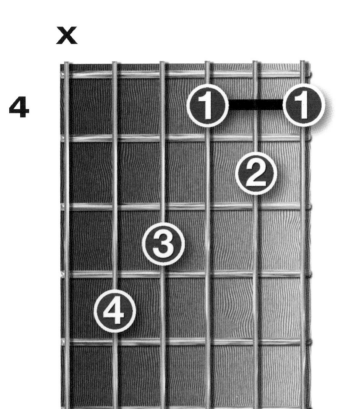

Chord Spelling
1st (E), 3rd (G♯), 5th (B)

FREE ACCESS on iPhone & Android etc, using any free QR code app

Scan to **HEAR** this chord, or go directly to flametreepublishing.com

START
HERE

THE
BASICS

A

A#/Bb

B

C

C#/Db

D

D#/Eb

E

F

F#/Gb

G

G#/Ab

CHORDS IN
CONTEXT

Em
Minor

(1st Position)

Chord Spelling
1st (E), b3rd (G), 5th (B)

FREE ACCESS on iPhone & Android
etc, using any free QR code app

Scan to **HEAR** this chord, or go directly
to flametreepublishing.com

Em
Minor
(**2nd** Position)

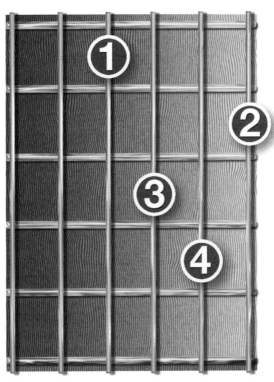

Chord Spelling
1st (E), ♭3rd (G), 5th (B)

START
HERE

THE
BASICS

A

A#/B♭

B

C

C#/D♭

D

D#/E♭

E

F

F#/G♭

G

G#/A♭

CHORDS IN
CONTEXT

Scan to **HEAR** this chord, or go directly to flametreepublishing.com

Esus4
Suspended 4th
(**1st** Position)

Chord Spelling
1st (E), 4th (A), 5th (B)

START HERE

THE BASICS

A

A#/Bb

B

C

C#/Db

D

D#/Eb

E

F

F#/Gb

G

G#/Ab

CHORDS IN CONTEXT

FREE ACCESS on iPhone & Android
etc, using any free QR code app

Scan to **HEAR** this chord, or go directly
to flametreepublishing.com

Emaj7
Major 7th

(**1st** Position)

START HERE

THE BASICS

A

A#/Bb

B

C

C#/Db

D

D#/Eb

E

F

F#/Gb

G

G#/Ab

CHORDS IN CONTEXT

Chord Spelling
1st (E), 3rd (G#), 5th (B), 7th (D#)

E7
Dominant 7th
(1st Position)

START
HERE

THE
BASICS

A

A#/Bb

B

C

C#/Db

D

D#/Eb

E

F

F#/Gb

G

G#/Ab

CHORDS IN
CONTEXT

Chord Spelling
1st (E), 3rd (G♯), 5th (B), ♭7th (D)

FREE ACCESS on iPhone & Android
etc, using any free QR code app

Scan to **HEAR** this chord, or go directly
to flametreepublishing.com

Em7
Minor 7th

(**1st** Position)

START
HERE

THE
BASICS

A

A#/Bb

B

C

C#/Db

D

D#/Eb

E

F

F#/Gb

G

G#/Ab

CHORDS IN
CONTEXT

Chord Spelling
1st (E), b3rd (G), 5th (B), b7th (D)

FREE ACCESS on iPhone & Android etc, using any free QR code app

Scan to **HEAR** this chord, or go directly to flametreepublishing.com

F
Major
(**1st** Position)

START
HERE

THE
BASICS

A

A#/Bb

B

C

C#/Db

D

D#/Eb

E

F

F#/Gb

G

G#/Ab

CHORDS IN
CONTEXT

Chord Spelling
1st (F), 3rd (A), 5th (C)

FREE ACCESS on iPhone & Android
etc, using any free QR code app

Scan to **HEAR** this chord, or go directly
to flametreepublishing.com

F
Major
(**2nd** Position)

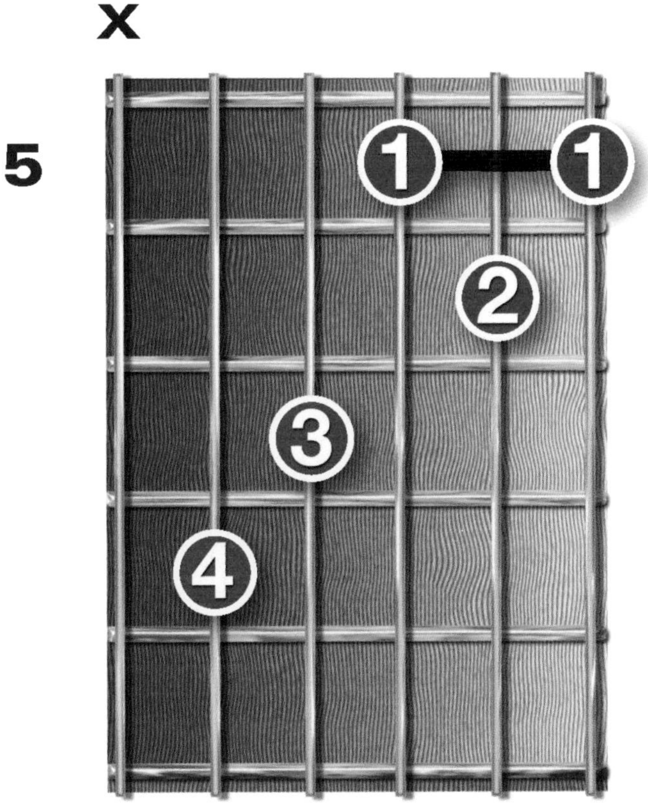

X

5

Chord Spelling
1st (F), 3rd (A), 5th (C)

START HERE

THE BASICS

A

A♯/B♭

B

C

C♯/D♭

D

D♯/E♭

E

F

F♯/G♭

G

G♯/A♭

CHORDS IN CONTEXT

Fm
Minor

(**1st** Position)

Chord Spelling

1st (F), ♭3rd (A♭), 5th (C)

Scan to **HEAR** this chord, or go directly
to flametreepublishing.com

START
HERE

THE
BASICS

A

A#/B♭

B

C

C#/D♭

D

D#/E♭

E

F

F#/G♭

G

G#/A♭

CHORDS IN
CONTEXT

Fm
Minor
(**2nd** Position)

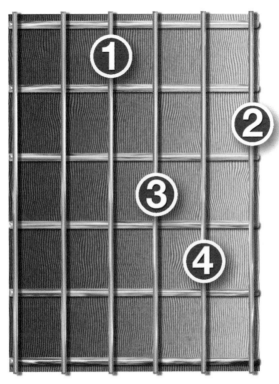

Chord Spelling
1st (F), ♭3rd (A♭), 5th (C)

FREE ACCESS on iPhone & Android etc, using any free QR code app

Scan to **HEAR** this chord, or go directly to flametreepublishing.com

Fsus4
Suspended 4th

(**1st** Position)

Chord Spelling
1st (F), 4th (Bb), 5th (C)

FREE ACCESS on iPhone & Android
etc, using any free QR code app

Scan to **HEAR** this chord, or go directly
to flametreepublishing.com

Fmaj7
Major 7th

(**1st** Position)

Chord Spelling
1st (F), 3rd (A), 5th (C), 7th (E)

START HERE

THE BASICS

A

A#/Bb

B

C

C#/Db

D

D#/Eb

E

F

F#/Gb

G

G#/Ab

CHORDS IN CONTEXT

Scan to **HEAR** this chord, or go directly to flametreepublishing.com

F7
Dominant 7th

(**1st** Position)

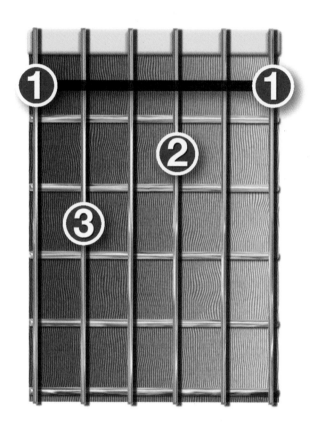

Chord Spelling
1st (F), 3rd (A), 5th (C), b7th (Eb)

FREE ACCESS on iPhone & Android
etc, using any free QR code app

Scan to **HEAR** this chord, or go directly
to flametreepublishing.com

Fm7
Minor 7th
(**1st** Position)

START
HERE

THE
BASICS

A

A#/B♭

B

C

C#/D♭

D

D#/E♭

E

F

F#/G♭

G

G#/A♭

CHORDS IN
CONTEXT

Chord Spelling
1st (F), ♭3rd (A♭), 5th (C), ♭7th (E♭)

FREE ACCESS on iPhone & Android etc,
using any free QR code app

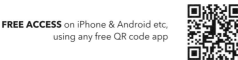

Scan to **HEAR** this chord, or go directly
to flametreepublishing.com

F♯/G♭
Major

(**1st** Position)

Chord Spelling
1st (F♯), 3rd (A♯), 5th (C♯)

FREE ACCESS on iPhone & Android
etc, using any free QR code app

Scan to **HEAR** this chord, or go directly
to flametreepublishing.com

START HERE

THE BASICS

A

A♯/B♭

B

C

C♯/D♭

D

D♯/E♭

E

F

F♯/G♭

G

G♯/A♭

CHORDS IN CONTEXT

F♯/G♭
Major
(2nd Position)

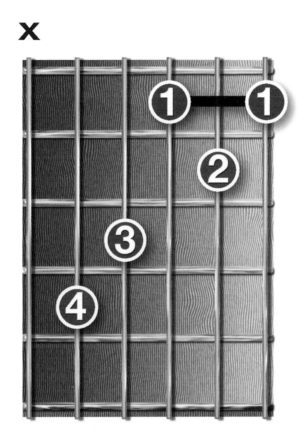

Chord Spelling
1st (F♯), 3rd (A♯), 5th (C♯)

Scan to **HEAR** this chord, or go directly to flametreepublishing.com

START HERE

THE BASICS

A

A♯/B♭

B

C

C♯/D♭

D

D♯/E♭

E

F

F♯/G♭

G

G♯/A♭

CHORDS IN CONTEXT

F♯/G♭m
Minor

(**1st** Position)

START
HERE

THE
BASICS

A

A♯/B♭

B

C

C♯/D♭

D

D♯/E♭

E

F

F♯/G♭

G

G♯/A♭

CHORDS IN
CONTEXT

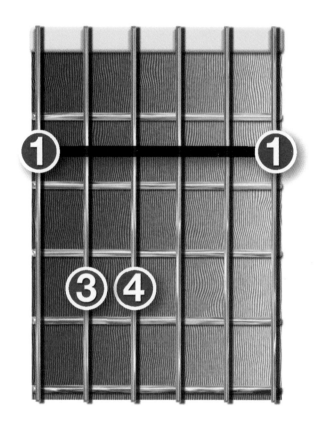

Chord Spelling
1st (F♯), ♭3rd (A), 5th (C♯)

FREE ACCESS on iPhone & Android
etc, using any free QR code app

Scan to **HEAR** this chord, or go directly
to flametreepublishing.com

F♯/G♭m
Minor
(**2nd** Position)

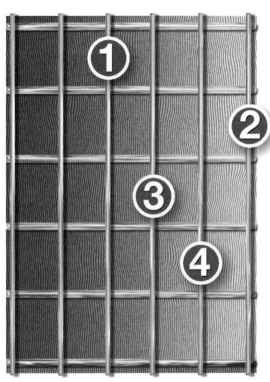

Chord Spelling
1st (F♯), ♭3rd (A), 5th (C♯)

FREE ACCESS on iPhone & Android etc, using any free QR code app

Scan to **HEAR** this chord, or go directly to flametreepublishing.com

F#/G♭sus4
Suspended 4th

(**1st** Position)

START
HERE

THE
BASICS

A

A#/B♭

B

C

C#/D♭

D

D#/E♭

E

F

F#/G♭

G

G#/A♭

CHORDS IN
CONTEXT

Chord Spelling
1st (F#), 4th (B), 5th (C#)

FREE ACCESS on iPhone & Android
etc, using any free QR code app

Scan to **HEAR** this chord, or go directly
to flametreepublishing.com

F♯/G♭maj7
Major 7th
(**1st** Position)

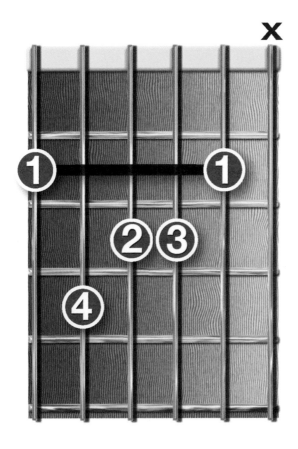

Chord Spelling
1st (F♯), 3rd (A♯), 5th (C♯), 7th (F)

Scan to **HEAR** this chord, or go directly to flametreepublishing.com

117

F#/Gb7
Dominant 7th
(1st Position)

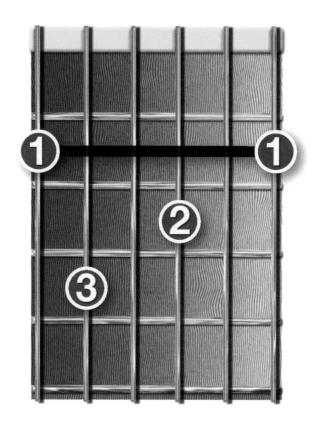

Chord Spelling
1st (F#), 3rd (A#), 5th (C#), b7th (E)

FREE ACCESS on iPhone & Android etc, using any free QR code app

Scan to **HEAR** this chord, or go directly to flametreepublishing.com

F♯/G♭m7
Minor 7th

(**1st** Position)

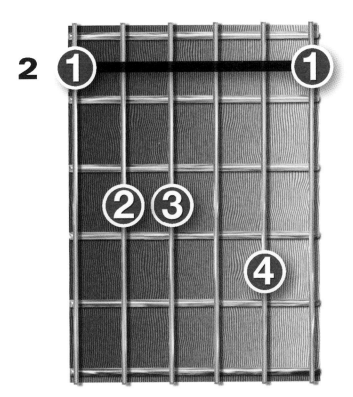

Chord Spelling
1st (F♯), ♭3rd (A), 5th (C♯), ♭7th (E)

START
HERE

THE
BASICS

A

A♯/B♭

B

C

C♯/D♭

D

D♯/E♭

E

F

F♯/G♭

G

G♯/A♭

CHORDS IN
CONTEXT

G
Major
(**1st** Position)

START
HERE

THE
BASICS

A

A#/Bb

B

C

C#/Db

D

D#/Eb

E

F

F#/Gb

G

G#/Ab

CHORDS IN
CONTEXT

Chord Spelling
1st (G), 3rd (B), 5th (D)

FREE ACCESS on iPhone & Android
etc, using any free QR code app

Scan to **HEAR** this chord, or go directly
to flametreepublishing.com

G
Major
(**2nd** Position)

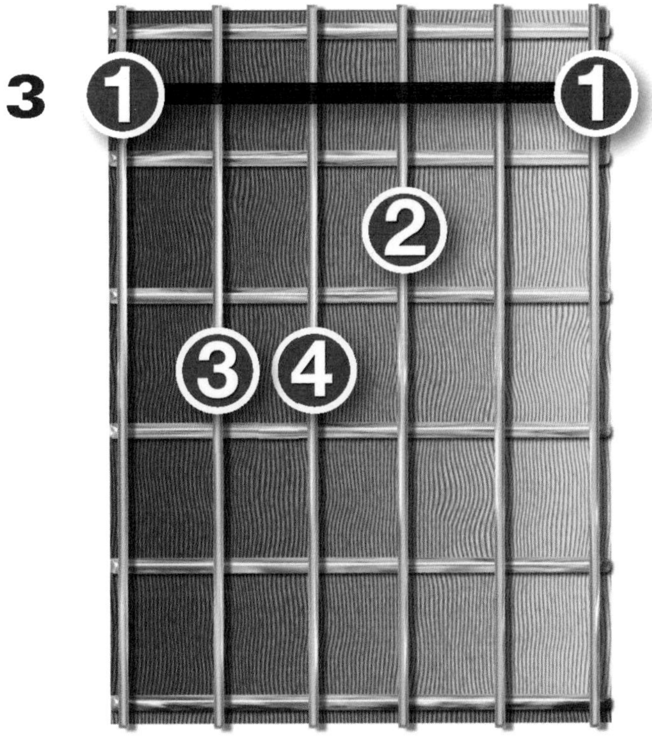

3 ① ① ① ② ③ ④

Chord Spelling
1st (G), 3rd (B), 5th (D)

START
HERE

THE
BASICS

A

A#/Bb

B

C

C#/Db

D

D#/Eb

E

F

F#/Gb

G

G#/Ab

CHORDS IN
CONTEXT

Gm
Minor
(**1st** Position)

START
HERE

THE
BASICS

A

A#/Bb

B

C

C#/Db

D

D#/Eb

E

F

F#/Gb

G

G#/Ab

CHORDS IN
CONTEXT

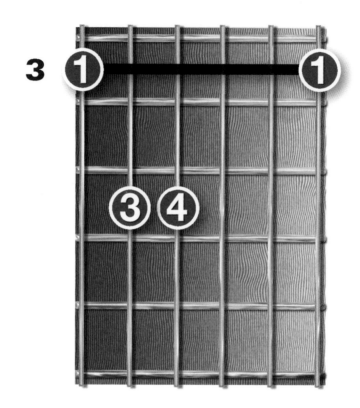

Chord Spelling
1st (G), b3rd (Bb), 5th (D)

FREE ACCESS on iPhone & Android
etc, using any free QR code app

Scan to **HEAR** this chord, or go directly
to flametreepublishing.com

Gm
Minor

(**2nd** Position)

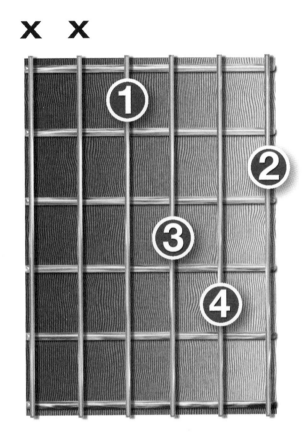

5

Chord Spelling
1st (G), ♭3rd (B♭), 5th (D)

Scan to **HEAR** this chord, or go directly to flametreepublishing.com

START HERE

THE BASICS

A

A♯/B♭

B

C

C♯/D♭

D

D♯/E♭

E

F

F♯/G♭

G

G♯/A♭

CHORDS IN CONTEXT

Gsus4
Suspended 4th

(**1st** Position)

Chord Spelling
1st (G), 4th (C), 5th (D)

FREE ACCESS on iPhone & Android etc, using any free QR code app

Scan to **HEAR** this chord, or go directly to flametreepublishing.com

Gmaj7
Major 7th

(**1st** Position)

START
HERE

THE
BASICS

A

A#/B♭

B

C

C#/D♭

D

D#/E♭

E

F

F#/G♭

G

G#/A♭

CHORDS IN
CONTEXT

X X

2

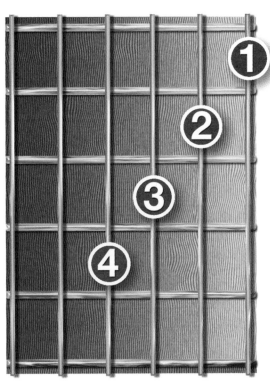

Chord Spelling
1st (G), 3rd (B), 5th (D), 7th (F♯)

G7
Dominant 7th

(**1st** Position)

START
HERE

THE
BASICS

A

A#/B♭

B

C

C#/D♭

D

D#/E♭

E

F

F#/G♭

G

G#/A♭

CHORDS IN
CONTEXT

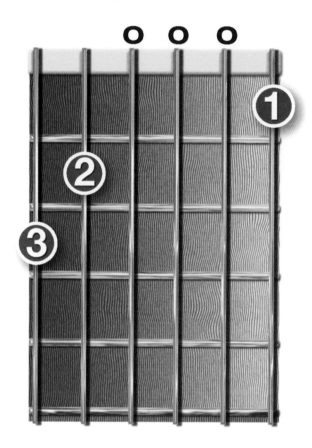

Chord Spelling
1st (G), 3rd (B), 5th (D), ♭7th (F)

FREE ACCESS on iPhone & Android
etc, using any free QR code app

Scan to **HEAR** this chord, or go directly
to flametreepublishing.com

126

Gm7
Minor 7th

(**1st** Position)

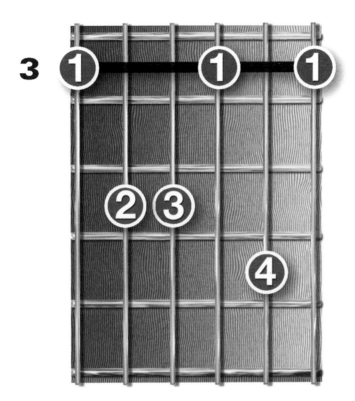

3

Chord Spelling
1st (G), ♭3rd (B♭), 5th (D), ♭7th (F)

START HERE

THE BASICS

A

A♯/B♭

B

C

C♯/D♭

D

D♯/E♭

E

F

F♯/G♭

G

G♯/A♭

CHORDS IN CONTEXT

FREE ACCESS on iPhone & Android etc, using any free QR code app

Scan to **HEAR** this chord, or go directly to flametreepublishing.com

G♯/A♭
Major

(**1st** Position)

START
HERE

THE
BASICS

A

A♯/B♭

B

C

C♯/D♭

D

D♯/E♭

E

F

F♯/G♭

G

G♯/A♭

CHORDS IN
CONTEXT

Chord Spelling
1st (A♭), 3rd (C), 5th (E♭)

FREE ACCESS on iPhone & Android
etc, using any free QR code app

Scan to **HEAR** this chord, or go directly
to flametreepublishing.com

G♯/A♭
Major
(2nd Position)

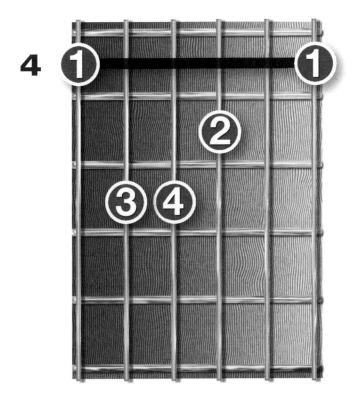

4

Chord Spelling
1st (A♭), 3rd (C), 5th (E♭)

Scan to **HEAR** this chord, or go directly to flametreepublishing.com

G♯/A♭m
Minor

(**1st** Position)

Chord Spelling
1st (A♭), ♭3rd (C♭), 5th (E♭)

FREE ACCESS on iPhone & Android etc, using any free QR code app

Scan to **HEAR** this chord, or go directly to flametreepublishing.com

START HERE

THE BASICS

A

A♯/B♭

B

C

C♯/D♭

D

D♯/E♭

E

F

F♯/G♭

G

G♯/A♭

CHORDS IN CONTEXT

G♯/A♭m
Minor
(**2nd** Position)

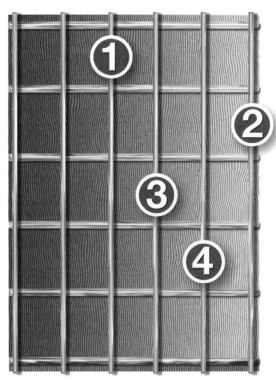

START HERE

THE BASICS

A

A♯/B♭

B

C

C♯/D♭

D

D♯/E♭

E

F

F♯/G♭

G

G♯/A♭

CHORDS IN CONTEXT

Chord Spelling
1st (A♭), ♭3rd (C♭), 5th (E♭)

FREE ACCESS on iPhone & Android etc, using any free QR code app

Scan to **HEAR** this chord, or go directly to flametreepublishing.com

131

G#/A♭sus4
Suspended 4th

(**1st** Position)

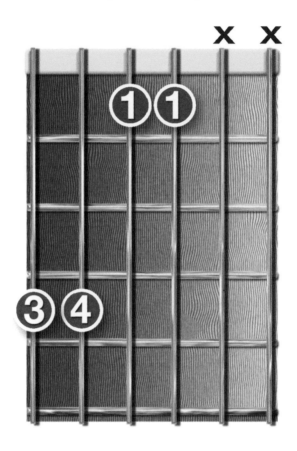

Chord Spelling
1st (A♭), 4th (D♭), 5th (E♭)

Scan to **HEAR** this chord, or go directly
to flametreepublishing.com

START HERE

THE BASICS

A

A#/B♭

B

C

C#/D♭

D

D#/E♭

E

F

F#/G♭

G

G#/A♭

CHORDS IN CONTEXT

G♯/A♭maj7
Major 7th

(**1st** Position)

3

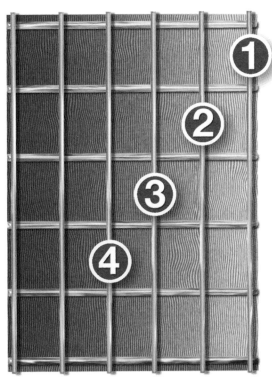

Chord Spelling
1st (A♭), 3rd (C), 5th (E♭), 7th (G)

G♯/A♭

Scan to **HEAR** this chord, or go directly to flametreepublishing.com

G♯/A♭7
Dominant 7th

(**1st** Position)

Chord Spelling
1st (A♭), 3rd (C), 5th (E♭), ♭7th (G♭)

FREE ACCESS on iPhone & Android
etc, using any free QR code app

Scan to **HEAR** this chord, or go directly
to flametreepublishing.com

G♯/A♭m7
Minor 7th

(1st Position)

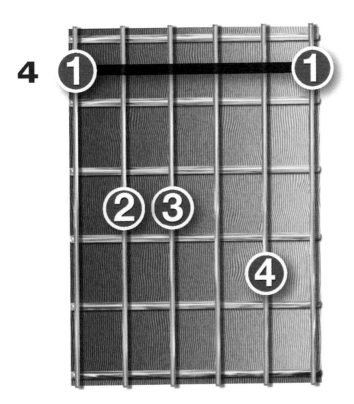

4

Chord Spelling
1st (A♭), ♭3rd (C♭), 5th (E♭), ♭7th (G♭)

START HERE

THE BASICS

A

A♯/B♭

B

C

C♯/D♭

D

D♯/E♭

E

F

F♯/G♭

G

G♯/A♭

CHORDS IN CONTEXT

Chords in Context

START
HERE

THE
BASICS

A

A#/Bb

B

C

C#/Db

D

D#/Eb

E

F

F#/Gb

G

G#/Ab

CHORDS IN
CONTEXT

Once you're familiar with the common chords shown in the chord section, the next step is to learn how to properly use and combine them to create great music.

In this chapter you will find more advanced techniques, aimed to build on the basic skills and theory outlined in the first section of this book. As well as advice on putting chords together, you'll find examples of chord progressions to help get you started with popular chord combinations in any key. It's possible to use the main chords in loads of different ways too, so we've included tips on developing your own playing style and experimenting with different sounds using just a few chords. And, if you're hungry for more chord types, you can learn about augmented and diminished triads, sus2 chords, power chords, 6th chords, altered chords and extended chords (9ths, 11ths, 13ths etc) to really expand your chord vocabulary.

This section will cover:

- **Techniques for smooth chord transitions**
- **Basic chord charts explained**
- **An example of a common chord progression in C**
- **Using the chord progression in other common keys**
- **Incorporating 7th chords**
- **Other variations on the common chord sequence**
- **Stylistic choices and ways to play the same chords**
- **Possible chord inversions, shown with C major**
- **An introduction to more advanced chords**

FREE ACCESS on iPhone & Android etc, using any free QR code app

Scan to **HEAR** the C major chord, and access the full library of scales and chords on flametreemusic.com

Scan to **HEAR** the C major chord, and access the full library of scales and chords on flametreemusic.com

CHORDS IN CONTEXT

START
HERE

THE
BASICS

A

A#/B♭

B

C

C#/D♭

D

D#/E♭

E

F

F#/G♭

G

G#/A♭

CHORDS IN
CONTEXT

Combining Chords

Now that you know a few chord shapes, it's important to learn how to change fluently between them without leaving gaps. This can be a difficult skill to master, but luckily there are a few shortcuts you can take to make your chord changes easier and faster.

Minimum Movement Principle

It's essential that chord changes are crisp, prompt, and in time. This can be made easier if following the '**minimum movement principle**', which involves making only the smallest finger movement necessary between chords, and avoiding taking fingers off strings or frets only to put them back on again for the next chord.

Excess movement between chords is what slows chord changes down; the less your fingers move, the faster your chord changes will be.

Shared Notes

Always look for links, or **common notes**, between consecutive chords, so you can minimize the amount of finger movement needed when changing chords. You may be able to keep some fingers on, or at least slide them along a string to the next chord.

Opposite you'll see a chord progression in A minor. Between each new chord there's a return to the basic A minor chord.

Notice the common notes between the chords shown: the first finger stays on the first fret and the second finger stays on the second fret throughout.

FREE ACCESS on iPhone & Android
etc, using any free QR code app

Scan to **HEAR** the C major chord, and
access the full library of scales and
chords on flametreemusic.com

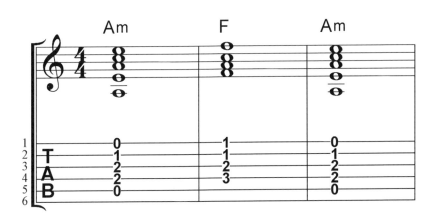

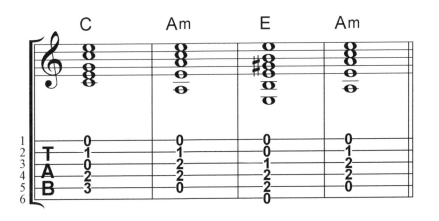

- The open position A minor and F major chords both include the note C (first fret on the B string).

- The C major chord also includes this note, and, in addition, has another note in common with the A minor chord (E on the second fret of the D string). Between Am and C only the third finger needs to be moved.

- Notice, too, how E major is the same 'shape' as Am – just on different strings.

Scan to **HEAR** the C major chord, and access the full library of scales and chords on flametreemusic.com

START HERE

THE BASICS

A

A#/Bb

B

C

C#/Db

D

D#/Eb

E

F

F#/Gb

G

G#/Ab

CHORDS IN CONTEXT

START
HERE

THE
BASICS

A

A#/Bb

B

C

C#/Db

D

D#/Eb

E

F

F#/Gb

G

G#/Ab

Power Chords

In rock music, instead of full chords, abbreviated versions just using the **root** and **fifth** note are often played. Apart from the tone, one of the main advantages of using these 'power chords' is that it's much easier to move quickly from chord to chord because there are only a couple of fingers involved.

To play a fifth power chord, simply fret a note on any bass string and add a note two frets up on the adjacent higher string. You can find examples of power chords on page 163.

Sliding Chords

The guitar is one of the few instruments on which you can **slide** chords up and down, changing their pitch easily and smoothly. The technique creates a fluidity and smoothness of sound. For more information on barre chords, see pages 38–39.

'Open Vamp' Strum

If all else fails, this is a 'pro-trick' you can use that will mask any gap between chord changes. It simply involves **strumming the open strings** while your fingers move between the chord change. While not ideal, it does mean that the overall fluency and momentum of the performance is maintained.

Opposite is an easy combination to start with. Remember:

- **Look for any links between the different chords.**
- **Place the fingers for each complete chord shape on the fretboard together, rather than finger by finger.**
- **Practise very slowly so that you don't develop a habit of slowing down or stopping between chord changes.**

CHORDS IN
CONTEXT

FREE ACCESS on iPhone & Android etc, using any free QR code app

Scan to **HEAR** the C major chord, and access the full library of scales and chords on flametreemusic.com

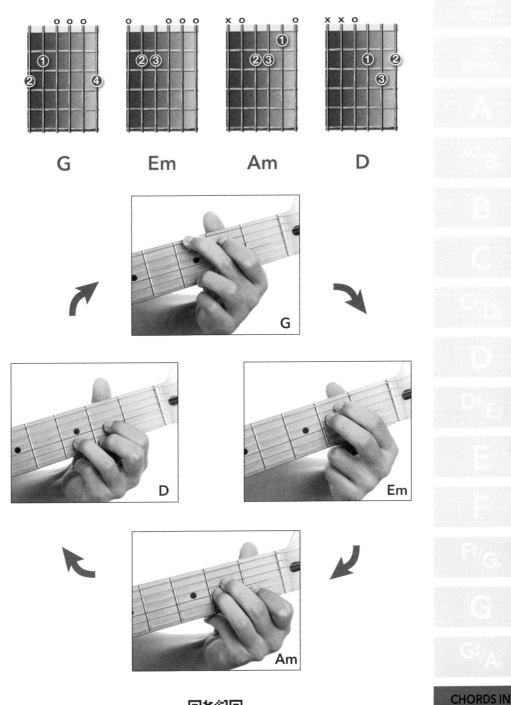

G   Em   Am   D

Chord Charts

Chord charts are a handy way to **communicate** information to other players, and also good for your own reference if you come up with a good combination of chords that you'll want to return to later.

Simple chord charts are the most common way of notating the chord structure of a song or chord progression. In their most basic form, chord charts usually include:

- **Vertical lines to indicate the start of a new measure**
- **Chord symbols to show which chords should be played**
- **Slash symbols signifying repeat chords**

For example:

|C / / /|G / / /|

This would mean the C major chord is played four times, followed by four G major chords.

If there is no **time signature** specified then it's usually safe to assume that the music is in 4/4 time. So for the above you could play the C major chord four times over 4 beats, followed by the G major chord four times over 4 beats.

When more than one chord appears in a single measure it can be assumed that the measure is to be **evenly** between the chords.

On the following pages common combinations of four chords are shown using chord charts.

START HERE

THE BASICS

A

A#/Bb

B

C

C#/Db

D

D#/Eb

E

F

F#/Gb

G

G#/Ab

CHORDS IN CONTEXT

Scan to **HEAR** the C major chord, and access the full library of scales and chords on flametreemusic.com

CHORDS IN CONTEXT

Common Chord Combinations

After learning the basic chords, the next step towards playing great music is knowing which chords sound well together. Over the following pages we'll introduce a common chord progression to help get you started with putting chords together.

An incredibly popular chord progression is the **I V vi IV** progression.

To work out which chords these refer to in C major, we can look again at the C major scale:

$$C \quad D \quad E \quad F \quad G \quad A \quad B$$

$$I \quad ii \quad iii \quad IV \quad V \quad vi \quad vii°$$

For a reminder of which types of chords are represented by these roman numerals, see pages 18–19.

The **I V vi IV** progression in C, therefore, would use the following chords:

$$C \qquad G \qquad Am \qquad F$$

$$I \qquad V \qquad vi \qquad IV$$

C major   G major   A minor   F major

This could be shown as a chord chart, in standard 4/4 time (four beats per bar):

| C / / / | G / / / | Am / / / | F / / / |

Sidebar navigation:
START HERE
THE BASICS
A
A#/Bb
B
C
C#/Db
D
D#/Eb
E
F
F#/Gb
G
G#/Ab
CHORDS IN CONTEXT

FREE ACCESS on iPhone & Android etc, using any free QR code app

Scan to **HEAR** the C major chord, and access the full library of scales and chords on flametreemusic.com

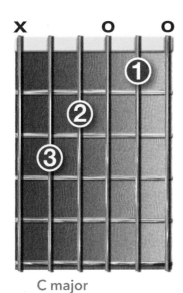

C major

Chord Spelling

1st (C), 3rd (E), 5th (G)

G major

Chord Spelling

1st (G), 3rd (B), 5th (D)

A minor

Chord Spelling

1st (A), ♭3rd (C), 5th (E)

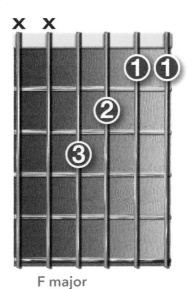

F major

Chord Spelling

1st (F), 3rd (A), 5th (C)

FREE ACCESS on iPhone & Android etc, using any free QR code app

Scan to **HEAR** the C major chord, and access the full library of scales and chords on flametreemusic.com

START HERE

THE BASICS

A

A♯/B♭

B

C

C♯/D♭

D

D♯/E♭

E

F

F♯/G♭

G

G♯/A♭

CHORDS IN CONTEXT

START
HERE

THE
BASICS

A

A#/B♭

B

C

C#/D♭

D

D#/E♭

E

F

F#/G♭

G

G#/A♭

In Other Keys

When chords and chord progressions are described in terms of roman numerals, they can be understood in terms of any key. The **I V vi IV** progression shown in C on pages 144–45 can therefore be applied to other keys.

After C major, some of the other most common keys include D major, E major, G major and A major. Here, we'll show which chords are needed in each of these keys to produce **I V vi IV**. The chord diagrams for these will follow on pages 148–151.

D Major
In D major, the chords needed for the **I V vi IV** progression are formed using the notes of the D major scale:

D   E   F♯   G   A   B   C♯

I   ii   iii   IV   V   vi   vii°

So the **I V vi IV** combination of chords in D major could be played as:

|D / / / | A / / / | Bm / / / | G / / / |

E Major
In E major, the chords needed for the **I V vi IV** progression are formed using the notes of the E major scale:

E   F♯   G♯   A   B   C♯   D♯

I   ii   iii   IV   V   vi   vii°

So the **I V vi IV** combination of chords in E major could be played as:

|E / / / | B / / / | C#m / / / | A / / / |

G Major
In G major, the chords needed for the **I V vi IV** progression are formed using the notes of the G major scale:

G A B C D E F#

I ii iii IV V vi vii°

So the **I V vi IV** combination of chords in D major could be played as:

|G / / / | D / / / | Em / / / | C / / / |

A Major
In A major, the chords needed for the **I V vi IV** progression are formed using the notes of the A major scale:

A B C# D E F# G#

I ii iii IV V vi vii°

So the **I V vi IV** combination of chords in D major could be played as:

|A / / / | E / / / | F#m / / / | D / / / |

CHORDS IN CONTEXT

I V vi IV in D major

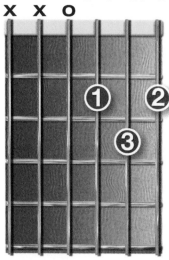

D major

Chord Spelling

1st (D), 3rd (F#), 5th (A)

A major

Chord Spelling

1st (A), 3rd (C#), 5th (E)

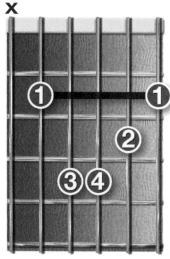

B minor

Chord Spelling

1st (B), b3rd (D), 5th (F#)

G major

Chord Spelling

1st (G), 3rd (B), 5th (D)

FREE ACCESS on iPhone & Android
etc, using any free QR code app

Scan to **HEAR** the C major chord, and
access the full library of scales and
chords on flametreemusic.com

I V vi IV in E major

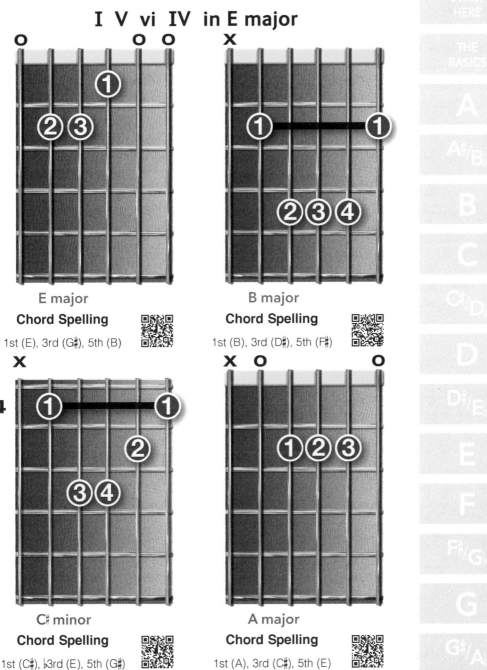

E major

Chord Spelling

1st (E), 3rd (G#), 5th (B)

B major

Chord Spelling

1st (B), 3rd (D#), 5th (F#)

C# minor

Chord Spelling

1st (C#), b3rd (E), 5th (G#)

A major

Chord Spelling

1st (A), 3rd (C#), 5th (E)

FREE ACCESS on iPhone & Android etc, using any free QR code app

Scan to **HEAR** the C major chord, and access the full library of scales and chords on flametreemusic.com

I V vi IV in G major

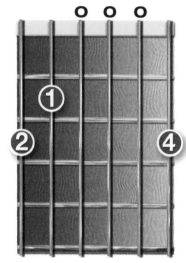

G major

Chord Spelling

1st (G), 3rd (B), 5th (D)

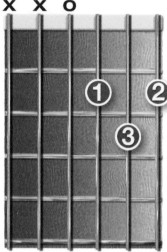

D major

Chord Spelling

1st (D), 3rd (F#), 5th (A)

E minor

Chord Spelling

1st (E), ♭3rd (G), 5th (B)

C major

Chord Spelling

1st (C), 3rd (E), 5th (G)

FREE ACCESS on iPhone & Android
etc, using any free QR code app

Scan to **HEAR** the C major chord, and
access the full library of scales and
chords on flametreemusic.com

Left sidebar navigation:
START HERE
THE BASICS
A
A#/B♭
B
C
C#/D♭
D
D#/E♭
E
F
F#/G♭
G
G#/A♭
CHORDS IN CONTEXT

I V vi IV in A major

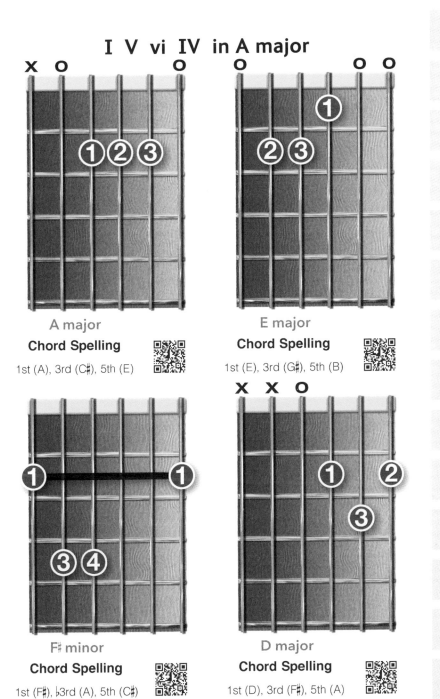

A major

Chord Spelling

1st (A), 3rd (C♯), 5th (E)

E major

Chord Spelling

1st (E), 3rd (G♯), 5th (B)

F♯ minor

Chord Spelling

1st (F♯), ♭3rd (A), 5th (C♯)

D major

Chord Spelling

1st (D), 3rd (F♯), 5th (A)

FREE ACCESS on iPhone & Android etc, using any free QR code app

Scan to **HEAR** the C major chord, and access the full library of scales and chords on flametreemusic.com

START
HERE

THE
BASICS

A

A#/B♭

B

C

C#/D♭

D

D#/E♭

E

F

F#/G♭

G

G#/A♭

CHORDS IN
CONTEXT

Variations

It's possible to rearrange the chords in any progression to produce new progressions. For example, some different combinations of the **I   V   vi   IV** could be:

- **I   vi   IV   V**
- **I   V   vi   IV**
- **vi   IV   I   V**
- **I   IV   vi   V**

These all use the same chords, but produce different musical effects when rearranged.

Other forms of variations when combining chords could be the substitution of other chord, or the embellishment of existing chords.

Adding 7ths

One of the most commonly used chord embellishments is the addition of a **7th** note, which is why we've included three types of 7th chords in this book:

- **major seventh (maj7)**
- **dominant seventh (7)**
- **minor seventh (m7)**

The dominant seventh versions of the I, IV and V chords are especially useful. Dominant 7ths use the major triad, but with an added **flattened 7th**.

In C major, these three chords would be C7, F7 and G7. We can use their relevant scales to find the 'seventh' note in each case:

C	D	E	F	G	A	B
F	G	A	B♭	C	D	E
G	A	B	C	D	E	F♯
I	ii	iii	IV	V	vi	vii°

So adding a flattened 7th to each of the chords gives us:

I	=	C	(C, E, G)
I7	**=**	**C7**	**(C, E, G, B♭)**
IV	=	F	(F, A, C)
IV7	**=**	**F7**	**(F, A, C, E♭)**
V	=	G	(G, B, D)
V7	**=**	**G7**	**(G, B, D, F)**

V7 chords are popular because all the notes in the chord can be found in the root key's major scale: here, all the notes in G7 are in the C major scale.

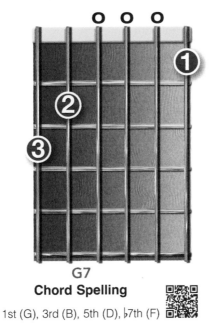

G7
Chord Spelling
1st (G), 3rd (B), 5th (D), ♭7th (F)

Scan to **HEAR** the C major chord, and access the full library of scales and chords on flametreemusic.com

START HERE

THE BASICS

A

A♯/B♭

B

C

C♯/D♭

D

D♯/E♭

E

F

F♯/G♭

G

G♯/A♭

CHORDS IN CONTEXT

Other Ways to Play Chords

There are many different ways of playing the same chord, so once you've got the basic chord shapes under control feel free to add some variety into your chord-playing.

Strum Patterns

Once you're familiar with chord changes and have mastered some of the basic strum patterns (see pages 36–37), try more combinations of down and upstrums.

You also don't need to strum all the strings, particularly when playing upstrums. Try the top two strings, or bottom two strings, rather than the whole chord. **Omitting** some bass strings on upstrokes and some treble strings on downstrokes will add variety too.

Remember, make sure your standing or sitting position doesn't restrict the movement of your hands and arms, and keep a **loose wrist action** for the fingers to move freely.

Have a go at this strum pattern, which alternates down- and upstrums.

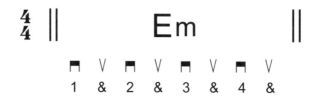

START HERE

THE BASICS

A

A#/Bb

B

C

C#/Db

D

D#/Eb

E

F

F#/Gb

G

G#/Ab

CHORDS IN CONTEXT

FREE ACCESS on iPhone & Android etc, using any free QR code app

Scan to **HEAR** the C major chord, and access the full library of scales and chords on flametreemusic.com

A
A♯/B♭
B
C
C♯/D♭
D
D♯/E♭
E
F
F♯/G♭
G
G♯/A♭

CHORDS IN
CONTEXT

FREE ACCESS on iPhone & Android etc, using any free QR code app

Scan to **HEAR** the C major chord, and access the full library of scales and chords on flametreemusic.com

START
HERE

THE
BASICS

A

A#/B♭

B

C

C#/D♭

D

D#/E♭

E

F

F#/G♭

G

G#/A♭

CHORDS IN
CONTEXT

Timing

Varying up the timing in your chord playing is one way to keep the sound interesting. For example, you can alter the number of strums per beat, or use a combination of short and long sounds, while still keeping a regular rhythm. In the example below, the chords are played with an identifiable rhythm: the chords with an extra bar across the top (semiquavers) are played in half the time of those with just one bar over the top (quavers).

With distortion.

Arpeggios

An arpeggio is a **broken chord** in which the notes of the chord are played individually (rather than strummed simultaneously). This can both reinforce the chord itself and lend an interesting pattern to the sounds.

When you're first learning arpeggios it's helpful to practise them in the set musical order they appear in the chord. Once you know the notes though you can **mix up** the order, or repeat some of the notes. You are also free to vary the **timing** between notes to create combinations of short and long note lengths. Practising arpeggios is also a good way to learn the individual notes that form a chord, as well as improve the **dexterity** of your guitar playing.

FREE ACCESS on iPhone & Android etc, using any free QR code app

Scan to **HEAR** the C major chord, and access the full library of scales and chords on flametreemusic.com

Below is an example of a C major arpeggio, shown first as a chord, then as the notes played separately. You can see that on the right the chord's notes are played individually in order: C, E, G and C again.

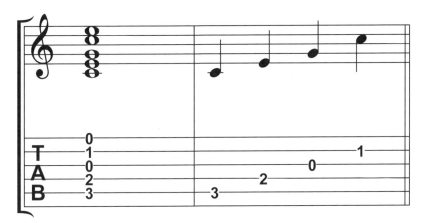

CHORDS IN CONTEXT

Chord Inversions

Rather than play every chord starting from its root note, you can play an 'inversion' by choosing another chord tone as the lowest note. There are three main types of inversion:

First Inversion: 3rd of the chord is the lowest note

Second Inversion: 5th of the chord is the lowest note

Third Inversion: extension of the chord is the lowest note

Inversions are normally notated as 'slash' chords:

C/E is 'C major first inversion'
The lowest note of this triad is E, with G and C above it.

C/G is 'C major second inversion'
The lowest note of this triad is G, with C and E above it.

Cmaj7/B is 'C major third inversion'
The lowest note of this chord is B, with C, E and G above it.

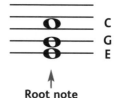

C Major 1st Inversion

3rd and 5th and octave notes
of the C Major scale

C
G
E

Root note

FREE ACCESS on iPhone & Android
etc, using any free QR code app

Scan to **HEAR** the C major chord, and
access the full library of scales and
chords on flametreemusic.com

158

START
HERE

THE
BASICS

A

A#/B♭

B

C

C#/D♭

D

D#/E♭

E

F

F#/G♭

G

G#/A♭

CHORDS IN
CONTEXT

C/E
C Major First Inversion

The notes in this chord are:
3rd (E), 5th (G), 1st (C)

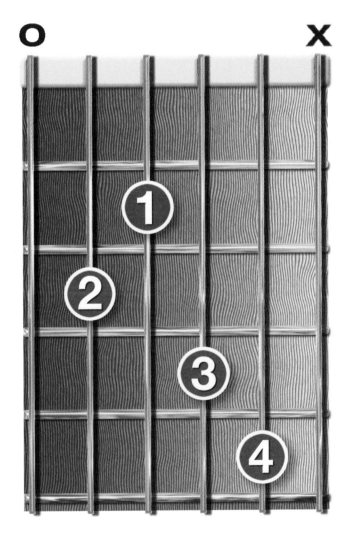

Scan to **HEAR** the C major chord, and access the full library of scales and chords on flametreemusic.com

CHORDS IN CONTEXT

C/G
C Major Second Inversion

The notes in this chord are:
5th (G), 1st (C), 3rd (E)

START
HERE

THE
BASICS

A

A#/B♭

B

C

C#/D♭

D

D#/E♭

E

F

F#/G♭

G

G#/A♭

CHORDS IN
CONTEXT

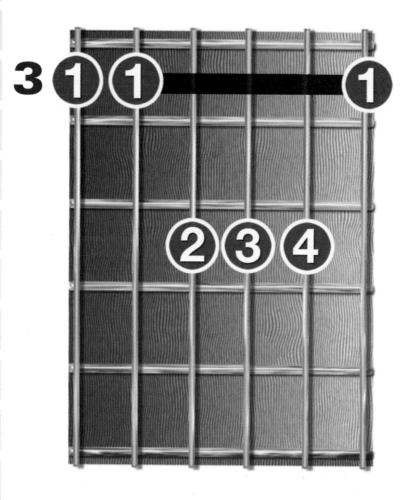

FREE ACCESS on iPhone & Android
etc, using any free QR code app

Scan to **HEAR** the C major chord, and
access the full library of scales and
chords on flametreemusic.com

Cmaj7/B
C Major Third Inversion

The notes in this chord are:
7th (B), 1st (C), 3rd (E), 5th (G)

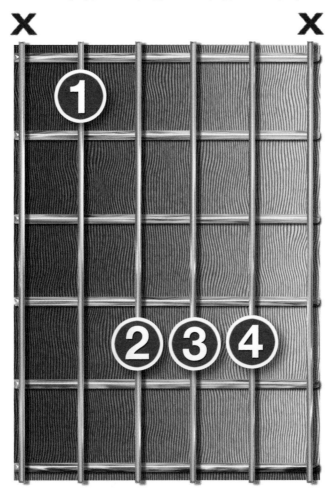

START HERE

THE BASICS

A

A#/Bb

B

C

C#/Db

D

D#/Eb

E

F

F#/Gb

G

G#/Ab

CHORDS IN CONTEXT

FREE ACCESS on iPhone & Android etc, using any free QR code app

Scan to **HEAR** the C major chord, and access the full library of scales and chords on flametreemusic.com

More Chords

This final section aims to introduce more chords into your repertoire. While that the chords already covered in this book are the ones you'll use the most, there are a few more types that it's useful to know about as they may crop up or come in handy during tricky chord combinations.

This section introduces the following more advanced chords:

- **Power Chords**
- **6th Chords**
- **Sus2 Chords**
- **Extended Chords: 9ths, 11ths and 13ths**
- **Altered Chords: Augmented and Diminished Triads, Diminished 7ths, and altered Dominant 7th chords (with flattened 5ths and flattened or sharpened 9ths)**

START HERE

THE BASICS

A

A#/B♭

B

C

C#/D♭

D

D#/E♭

E

F

F#/G♭

G

G#/A♭

CHORDS IN CONTEXT

FREE ACCESS on iPhone & Android etc, using any free QR code app

Scan to **HEAR** the C major chord, and access the full library of scales and chords on flametreemusic.com

Power Chords

Power chords unusually do not include a major or minor third; they consist only of the **root note** and the **fifth**. They are common in rock music, where the root note and the fifth above it are played on the sixth and fifth, or fifth and fourth strings. With the right combination of electric guitar, amp and effects, this powerful sound characterizes hard rock and heavy metal.

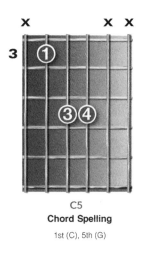

C5
Chord Spelling
1st (C), 5th (G)

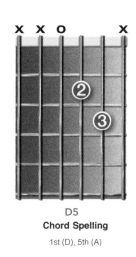

D5
Chord Spelling
1st (D), 5th (A)

E5
Chord Spelling
1st (E), 5th (B)

G5
Chord Spelling
1st (G), 5th (D)

A5
Chord Spelling
1st (A), 5th (E)

FREE ACCESS on iPhone & Android etc, using any free QR code app

Scan to **HEAR** the C major chord, and access the full library of scales and chords on flametreemusic.com

CHORDS IN CONTEXT

START
HERE

THE
BASICS

A

A#/B♭

B

C

C#/D♭

D

D#/E♭

E

F

F#/G♭

G

G#/A♭

CHORDS IN
CONTEXT

6th Chords

This involves the sixth note of the major scale. For example, in C major:

C   D   E   F   G   A   B   C

A C6 chord (C major 6th) would consist of the regular C major triad notes:
C, E, G, plus the sixth note of the major scale: A.

Minor sixth chords are formed in the same way, with the sixth note of the major scale added to the minor triad. **So Cm6 would be: C, E♭, G, A.**

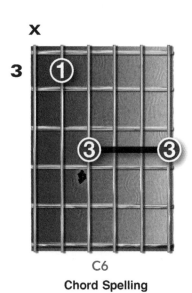

C6
Chord Spelling
1st (C), 3rd (E), 5th (G), 6th (A)

Cm6
Chord Spelling
1st (C), ♭3rd (E♭), 5th (G), 6th (A)

FREE ACCESS on iPhone & Android
etc, using any free QR code app

Scan to **HEAR** the C major chord, and
access the full library of scales and
chords on flametreemusic.com

Sus chords

Sus chords are formed by **replacing** a note, rather than adding one. As well as the sus4 chords shown in this book, there are **sus2** chords: in sus2 chords, it is the second note of the scale that replaces the chord's third.

If you lift the finger of the first string when playing an open position D major chord shape, it will become a **Dsus2** chord.

D major

Chord Spelling

1st (D), 3rd (F♯), 5th (A)

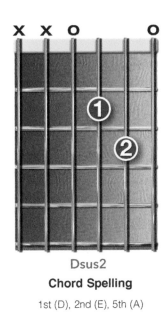

Dsus2

Chord Spelling

1st (D), 2nd (E), 5th (A)

Extended Chords

Extended chords contain more notes. Just as 7th chords are built by adding an extra note to a basic triad, extended chords are built by adding one or more extra notes to a 7th chord. The most common types of extended chords are 9ths, 11ths and 13ths. Each can be played in either a major, minor or dominant form.

CHORDS IN CONTEXT

START HERE

THE BASICS

A

A♯/B♭

B

C

C♯/D♭

D

D♯/E♭

E

F

F♯/G♭

G

G♯/A♭

START
HERE

THE
BASICS

A

A#/Bb

B

C

C#/Db

D

D#/Eb

E

F

F#/Gb

G

G#/Ab

CHORDS IN
CONTEXT

Cmaj9

Major 9th

9th chords add the 9th note of the scale to the regular chord. Major 9th chords have a delicate sound that makes them highly suitable for use in ballads. They are extensions of major 7th chords, and are formed by adding the ninth note of the major scale (with the same starting note).

Cmaj9 contains the notes of **Cmaj7**: C E G B; plus the **ninth** note of the C major scale: **D**.

so **Cmaj9** is **C E G B D**

C9

Dominant 9th

Dominant 9th chords have a rich, bluesy sound. They are formed by adding the ninth note of the major scale to a dominant 7th chord.

C9 contains the notes of **C7**: C E G Bb; plus the **ninth** note of the C major scale: **D**.

so **C9** is **C E G Bb D**

Minor 9th

Minor 9th chords have a suave, mellow sound and are often used in soul and funk music. They are extensions of minor seventh chords, formed by adding the ninth note of the major scale.

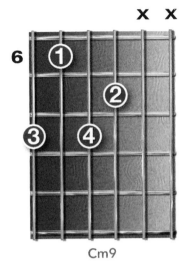

Cm9

Cm9 contains the notes of **Cm7**: C E♭ G B♭; plus the ninth note of the C major scale: **D**.

so **Cm9** is **C E♭ G B♭ D**

Cadd9

The ninth note can also be added to a simple triad, as this creates a certain warmth when added to a basic major chord.

Cadd9 uses the basic **C major chord**: C E G; plus the ninth note of the C major scale: **D**.

so **Cadd9** is **C E G D**

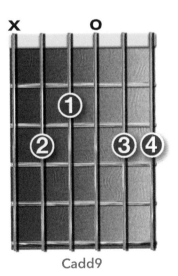

Cadd9

Scan to **HEAR** the C major chord, and access the full library of scales and chords on flametreemusic.com

CHORDS IN CONTEXT

START HERE

THE BASICS

A

A♯/B♭

B

C

C♯/D♭

D

D♯/E♭

E

F

F♯/G♭

G

G♯/A♭

START
HERE

THE
BASICS

A

A#/B♭

B

C

C#/D♭

D

D#/E♭

E

F

F#/G♭

G

G#/A♭

CHORDS IN
CONTEXT

Major 11th

11th chords extend chords even further, by adding the 11th note on top of a ninth chord. For example, using the C major scale:

C   D   E   F   G   A   B   C   D   E   F

So **Cmaj11** is: **C E G B D F**

In practice, the ninth note is normally omitted when playing 11th chords on the guitar.

Cmaj11

Dominant 11th

Dominant 11th chords are formed by adding the 11th note of the major scale to a dominant 7th or dominant 9th chord.

C11 contains the notes of **C9**: C E G B♭ D; plus the eleventh note of the C major scale: **F**.

So **C11** is: **C E G B♭ D F**

C11

Minor 11th

Minor 11th chords are formed by adding the 11th note of the major scale to a minor 7th or minor 9th chord.

Cm11 contains the notes of **Cm9**: C E♭ G B♭ D; plus the eleventh note of the C major scale: **F**.

So **Cm11** is: **C E♭ G B♭ D F**

Cm11

START HERE

THE BASICS

A

A#/B♭

B

C

C#/D♭

D

D#/E♭

E

F

F#/G♭

G

G#/A♭

CHORDS IN CONTEXT

FREE ACCESS on iPhone & Android etc, using any free QR code app

Scan to **HEAR** the C major chord, and access the full library of scales and chords on flametreemusic.com

START
HERE

THE
BASICS

A

A#/B♭

B

C

C#/D♭

D

D#/E♭

E

F

F#/G♭

G

G#/A♭

CHORDS IN
CONTEXT

Major 13th

As with 9th and 11th chords, there are 3 main types of 13th chords too: major, dominant and minor versions. Each follows the same technique, using the core triad, and adding the 7th, 9th, 11th and now 13th note above. For example, using the C major scale:

C D E F G A B C D E F G A

So **Cmaj13 is: C E G B D F A**

In practice, it is not possible to play all seven notes of a 13th chord on a guitar, therefore some notes (normally the 9th, 11th and sometimes the 5th) are omitted.

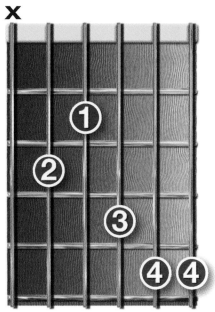

Cmaj13

FREE ACCESS on iPhone & Android
etc, using any free QR code app

Scan to **HEAR** the C major chord, and access the full library of scales and chords on flametreemusic.com

Dominant 13th

Dominant 13th chords are formed by adding the 13th note of the major scale to a dominant chord.

C13 contains the notes of **C11**: C E G B♭ D F; plus the 13th note of C major scale: **A**.

So **Cm11** is: **C E G B♭ D F A**

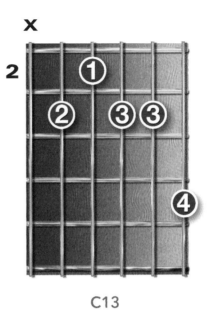

C13

Minor 13th

Minor 13th chords are formed by adding the 13th note of the major scale to a minor chord.

Cm13 contains the notes of **Cm11**: C E♭ G B♭ D F; plus the 13th note of the C major scale: **A**.

So **Cm13** is: **C E♭ G B♭ D F A**

Cm13

Scan to **HEAR** the C major chord, and access the full library of scales and chords on flametreemusic.com

CHORDS IN CONTEXT

START HERE

THE BASICS

A

A♯/B♭

B

C

C♯/D♭

D

D♯/E♭

E

F

F♯/G♭

G

G♯/A♭

START
HERE

THE
BASICS

A

A#/Bb

B

C

C#/Db

D

D#/Eb

E

F

F#/Gb

G

G#/Ab

CHORDS IN
CONTEXT

Altered Chords

Altered chords provide an ideal method of creating a sense of tension and adding harmonic dissonance to a chord progression.

Augmented triad:	**+**
Diminished triad:	**°**
Diminished 7th:	**°7**
Dominant 7th♭5:	**7♭5**
Dominant 7th♭9:	**7♭9**
Dominant 7th♯9:	**7♯9**

FREE ACCESS on iPhone & Android
etc, using any free QR code app

Scan to **HEAR** the C major chord, and access the full library of scales and chords on flametreemusic.com

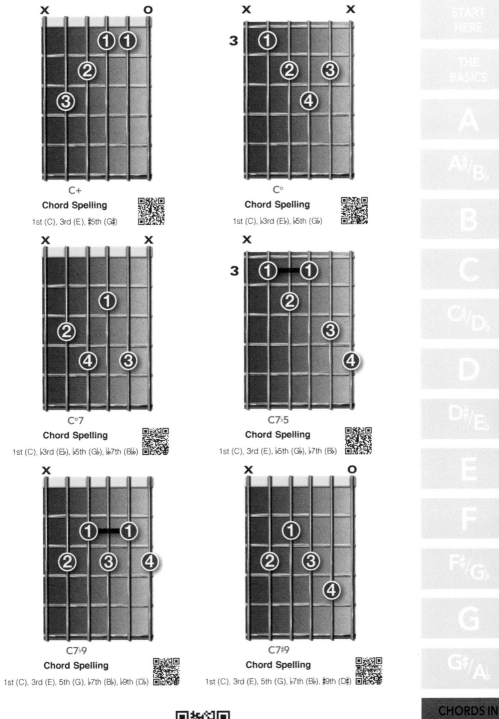

C+
Chord Spelling
1st (C), 3rd (E), ♯5th (G♯)

C°
Chord Spelling
1st (C), ♭3rd (E♭), ♭5th (G♭)

C°7
Chord Spelling
1st (C), ♭3rd (E♭), ♭5th (G♭), ♭♭7th (B♭♭)

C7♭5
Chord Spelling
1st (C), 3rd (E), ♭5th (G♭), ♭7th (B♭)

C7♭9
Chord Spelling
1st (C), 3rd (E), 5th (G), ♭7th (B♭), ♭9th (D♭)

C7♯9
Chord Spelling
1st (C), 3rd (E), 5th (G), ♭7th (B♭), ♯9th (D♯)

START HERE
THE BASICS
A
A♯/B♭
B
C
C♯/D♭
D
D♯/E♭
E
F
F♯/G♭
G
G♯/A♭
CHORDS IN CONTEXT

FREE ACCESS on iPhone & Android etc, using any free QR code app

Scan to **HEAR** the C major chord, and access the full library of scales and chords on flametreemusic.com

START
HERE

THE
BASICS

A

A#/B♭

B

C

C#/D♭

D

D#/E♭

E

F

F#/G♭

G

G#/A♭

CHORDS IN
CONTEXT

Resources

Here are a few companion titles that could come in useful if you intend to develop your skills playing and songwriting for the Guitar.

Guitar Chords Card Pack

This pack of cards introduces common chord structures and encourages experimentation with the most popular chords, with one clear guitar diagram per card.

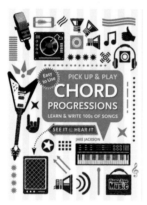

Chord Progressions

Take your chords to the next level with this book on popular chord combinations. Shows the chords in use with several examples, and diagrams for the all most useful chords and keys.

Classic Riffs: Licks & Riffs in the Style of Great Guitar Heroes

Over 70 riffs feature in this collection of riff styles. Play like Ritchie Blackmore, Jimmy Page, Slash, Kurt Cobain and more, with riffs written in standard notation and tablature.

FREE ACCESS on iPhone & Android etc, using any free QR code app

Scan to **HEAR** the C major chord, and access the full library of scales and chords on flametreemusic.com